D1563517

AFTER I WAS SIXTY

AFTER I WAS SIXTY

A Chapter of Autobiography

BY

LORD THOMSON
OF FLEET

NELSON

First published in Great Britain, 1975
by Hamish Hamilton Limited
90 Great Russell Street, London WC1
and simultaneously in Canada by
Thomas Nelson & Sons (Canada) Limited
81 Curlew Drive, Don Mills, Ontario M3A 2R1
Copyright © 1975 by Lord Thomson of Fleet

ISBN: 0-176-05008-6

Printed in Great Britain

Contents

List of Illustrations

vii

As Colonel-in-Chief of Toronto Scottish Regiment, with Queen Elizabeth the Queen Mother, during her Canadian tour, 1962

Greeting Princess Margaret at the Ritz, 1963, when H.R.H. presented the Ambassador Awards for Achievement

Illustrated London News 125th Anniversary: Mr. Gordon Brunton, with Lord Thomson, greets the Prime Minister, 1967

Foyle's luncheon, 1969: Lord Thomson welcomed by Mr. Hugh Cudlipp and Mr. Cecil King

IN PUTTING together this book I have resisted without any difficulty the temptation to write my life-story. These chapters are concerned only with what has happened to me since I came to Britain in 1954; my life in Canada before that was more than adequately and brilliantly covered by Russell Braddon in his 1965 biography.* Russell's book took in also about half of the British years. For that reason, and because I am by nature disinclined to indulge what someone called the last vanity of the autobiography, I have not attempted to make this a full account of these twenty years I've spent in Britain. I have missed out much—about some deals and about some of the people, to whom I hope I have already made plain my gratitude and affection (or the opposite).

But I have come to love Britain in these years and I wanted to put that down on paper. Since I was sixty I have been very fortunate in many ways: in making some fine friends, in meeting some fine people, great and small, and also in having a great success with my enter-prises. That success has sometimes astonished me. I came back to the land which an ancestor of mine left as an emigrant nearly two centuries ago, and my aim was not ambitious: simply to do some interesting but not too strenuous work so that I wouldn't be bored in my old age. I can tell you I have never been bored. A great many things have happened to and around me which almost any newspaper could be forgiven for calling 'momentous'.

* *Roy Thomson of Fleet Street*, Collins, 1965.

There is a second reason why I have felt I might assemble these memories and publish them. If I recall how some of the events came about, how some of that quite considerable success was achieved fairly late in my life, I may be of help or at least encouragement to younger people who still have, as I had, to try again.

These then are my recollections of some of the things that have happened in a very full twenty years. Mostly I have put them on tape in the last year or two and I am grateful to James Dow for researching into these past twenty years, verifying the things that were done and what was said, and helping me to put everything into good shape.

I DWELT IN MARBLE HALLS

MY FIRST venture into newspaper publishing was in 1934, and it was not until 1953, nineteen years later, that I flew into Edinburgh to buy control of a paper, my first in the United Kingdom: *The Scotsman*. So much has happened since that day, so much more than ever happened to me in Canada, that it is hard, even for me, to recollect that it all began when I was sixty.

To be exact in my sixtieth year, being fairly healthy and otherwise in my right mind, I was in Edinburgh looking for trouble. If I bought *The Scotsman* I would be starting a new career, one demanding an expenditure of energy, an unflagging spirit and long hours of hard work at an age when most men with any sense would be preparing for their retirement. I couldn't help asking myself: why did I want to do it?

I would be leaving behind a pretty comfortable existence. I had, by anyone's standards, been reasonably successful. I didn't think of myself as, nor was I regarded as a millionaire, but I dare say I could have scraped up a million or even two, if I had been pushed or if I'd wanted to. I had created a sound and solid Canadian business, unlike any other in the country, and I was making more money than I or my family would normally have spent, none of us having extravagant tastes. I had acquired in fact some sixteen newspapers and a small string of radio stations, which were all in smallish places practically unknown to people in Britain. I had made myself important enough in my own country to be elected president of Canadian Press for a year. What more did I want? It wasn't really a question of wanting anything.

It was the end of a great friendship and business partnership and the subsequent loss of my wife which together brought my life in Canada to a terminal point. I suffered deeply from both these events.

Jack Kent Cooke came to me for a job in November, 1936. He was a salesman with the Colgate-Palmolive Company; he was twenty-four and ambitious. I made him station manager at Stratford, Ontario, and he did a remarkable job in smoothing out all that station's difficulties and turning it, in six months, into a profitable concern. He was a man, I soon recognized, who had all the instincts and flair of a superb salesman. At that time, Wally Johnson, my accountant, had to do no more than call us up with the information that we were getting dangerously low at the bank and Jack would go out and sell enough business to float us. I made him my national sales boss in Toronto, where I had an office, too, and we became very friendly. Later I put him in charge of all the radio stations. I could hardly move quickly enough. Soon we were partners and he was getting his share of all the business deals we were putting through. For this arrangement we did not need to draw up a contract; we never even considered the necessity.

Jack and I were very much of a kind, enjoying the same jokes, going to the same shows, and getting most of our pleasure out of our work. He was the first one, apart from my wife, with whom I had been able to share my business hopes and plans. That in itself means a great deal; a man, in business as I was, is very much on his own; when he wins or when he gets hurt he can't turn to anyone who will properly understand and sympathize. No one complains about that: if you are pitting yourself against the pack, it is bound to be a lonely life, and if you find the sort of partner I did, you can't overcall his value. But then it happened that in 1949, after thirteen years of complete confidence and, I believed, complete understanding, our partnership came to an end. Jack told me he had been offered a 100,000 dollars a year contract to run one of the biggest radio stations in Canada and he had signed the deal, but that one condition he had been obliged to accept was that I would have no part in it. In none of our previous deals had such a condition been even considered. This, although nothing was said, was the parting of the ways. A year later we split completely both in our business and personal connections.

Within eighteen months I suffered the even greater blow of the death of my wife, after a brief illness. All my married life, I had spent a great deal of time away from my home; work for me had always meant long hours and often long journeys. When Edna moved from North Bay to Toronto because of the cruel winters, she rarely saw me except at weekends. Yet she had always known that, in spite of this separation, she remained of the utmost importance in my life. She had run the home and mothered the family so well and without fuss that my comings and goings, my lateness for meals, my uselessness about the house, none of these things were ever allowed to upset the straight and well-ordered pattern of life in which she brought up the children and kept things going for me, so that in whatever pickle I got myself in business, at my back there was constant calm and assurance and no worries. Besides that, I could always count on her hundred per cent support. Not once had she ever lost confidence in me, or hesitated in going forward where I wanted to go. If from time to time she asked, 'Why do you need more? Why not settle for what you've got?'

it was only to sound a note of caution; it was entirely because of her concern for me and her proper anxiety for the son who would take over from me. Now in January 1952 she was gone. At such a time a man realizes what he has sacrificed and neglected while he went in blinkers about his business.

This was a bleak period in my life. I threw myself into business activities but somehow nothing seemed the same. Now there was no one in whom I could confide, on whose understanding I could count. My two daughters were married and in their own homes; my son was at Galt learning the business and still too young to appreciate what made his old man tick. Besides Jack Kent Cooke, my partner, and Edna, my wife, there had been no one to share with me what went on in my mind.

I knew I had to get out of that rut. So I tried another card. I thought I might get into the Canadian Parliament and put myself forward as Conservative candidate for the Riding of York centre. I was adopted and I was defeated, thank Heaven.

In the spring of 1953 a correspondence began between me and Edinburgh and, when it was too late for me to withdraw from the election even if I had wanted to, a letter arrived informing me that I could have a share in the *Scotsman*, either small or large, whatever I wanted. I couldn't of course go over myself but I sent two of my top men to examine the proposition and the prospects, and I can tell you that if I had won the election, I would certainly have lost the *Scotsman*. They didn't say so then, but what they really wanted—and needed—was a resident proprietor. I would for the first time have missed a really good business opportunity, and this one, though of course I didn't know it then, was to be the greatest in my life.

So, in my sixtieth year, I was proposing to uproot myself from Canada and to begin afresh in a Scottish city which had a reputation for aloofness, where in any case I knew no one and no one knew me. Why did I want to do it? In my homeland I was leaving behind good friends of many years' standing, I was abandoning a pleasant way of life. I would be embarking on totally new experiences in a completely unknown country.

Why did I want to do it? Because all my life I have been worried when I have remained for a long time in a routine and settled way of daily habits. I was always afraid of standing still, of stagnating. My ambition had always kept well ahead of my accomplishments. The chance of becoming owner of a truly national newspaper in contrast to the purely local dailies which I ran in Canada—and indeed the *Scotsman* was a paper with an international reputation, an entirely different proposition from anything I owned—had a strong appeal.

I knew nothing of customs or business methods in Scotland. I had no knowledge of what I would have to face in the old country, but I was pretty sure it would be tough. I felt I could hold my own with almost anyone in a business deal in Canada, but there was more to this than a deal: did I have the ability to make a success of life in Scotland . . . on my own? Could I, the man from the Timmins Press, operate a national newspaper in a city where the standards of behaviour and the ways of commerce had been developed for three hundred years and more, along lines and rules and customs as unlike those of Canada as two countries of the same heritage could conceivably accomplish? My adult life, though I didn't know it then, was falling into three parts, three parts of almost equal length: a young manhood of some failure or rather of repeated non-success that lasted till I was forty; the second phase from forty-to-sixty with success coming at last; and then the curious urge to step into the top class, probably due to nothing more complex than the loss of my wife or, more probably, the break with my young partner, who had been compelled to separate from me in order, as his new associates said, to get into the big league. In the third twenty years I seem to have been showing him and those Canadians who told him, 'We don't want any part of Roy Thomson in this,' what the big league really means; whether or not this was what I was trying to do, perhaps subconsciously, I cannot say.

For at that time, in Edinburgh in 1953, I had no misgivings as to my ability to succeed in business there. Since I had broken through into the successful management of newspapers in Canada, never mind how small they were, I had begun to learn that I had considerable advantages. Most of the people who owned and ran newspapers in Canada and America and in Britain did so because they liked the prestige and the power that newspaper ownership gave them, or because they had inherited that ownership and, without a great deal of personal enthusiasm or in any case without devoting a great deal of energy, were keeping a family business ticking over. I, on the other hand, was wholly profit-orientated; I had learned a great deal from my few failures; I applied to the newspaper game strict business principles and no illusions; and I was industrious to a degree that ruled out weekend golf and other pursuits not likely to help in business. I always knew when I took over a paper that I could make it run better than the people from whom I bought it. I never had any doubt of that. Right through those twenty years of the great expansion, when we bought so many papers all over the world, I almost invariably felt that in each case we were taking over a newspaper that needed our help, that with better management would be a success, even a great success. It wasn't some figures I spotted in the balance sheet that made me think the paper in Edinburgh or anywhere else was a good buy, it was the figures that might have been there but weren't.

Let me tell you how the *Scotsman* came to be offered to me, of all people. During the 1946 Commonwealth Press Conference in Edinburgh, I met Colin Mackinnon, one of the partners of the *Scotsman* Publications Ltd. He came to Canada as a British delegate to the Commonwealth Press Union in 1950 and he was glad then that he knew me and we saw something of each other at that time. Then a year or two later, when I was in London, I came across his telephone number which, like a good North American businessman, I had kept for just this sort of opportunity, and I gave him a call. During our talk, I mentioned that I was interested in buying a British newspaper, and asked if he knew of one that might be looking for a buyer. He said that he didn't. I then had the impulse to ask him about the *Scotsman* itself, but of course I made the approach very carefully. Some newspapers are properties that can be bought and sold like any other business but a curiously high proportion of them are in their nature institutions or family businesses that have come to be regarded as trusts and the merest suggestion of an offer to purchase would be received like an insult. I guessed that this would be the case with the *Scotsman* and I didn't ask if it was likely ever to be sold but whether at any time any shares were ever likely to come up for sale. I was told very definitely that it was a family business, had been for more than a century, and no sale of its shares could take place. 'Well,' I said, unabashed, 'if any of the family ever want to sell any of their shares, will you give me the opportunity to talk about them?'

In February of that year, 1953, before starting on my election campaign, I thought again about how the idea had come to me of buying the *Scotsman* and settling in Edinburgh. Now I knew how anxious about death duties were the Findlay family, who had owned the *Scotsman* for over a hundred years. If anything happened to the chairman, Sir Edmund Findlay, the death duties would

7

make ravages in the finances of the newspaper, would more than likely force them to sell it, and it might get into wrong hands, a prospect which genuinely depressed and worried them. The more I thought about it, the more determined I became, and finally I wrote to Colin Mackinnon. The reply was emphatic. The *Scotsman* had belonged to the same family for all those years and it was not for sale in whole or in part, nor was it likely to be. There was something else behind that letter, though it was positive enough and no doubt truly represented what Colin and his partners thought. But were they not burying their heads in the sand? Well, there was nothing I could do more than let them know they had a crazy Canadian ready to buy from them. As it happened, that letter was the crucial step for me and for them.

Having been rebuffed, I turned my thoughts to a bank in Florida. I had spent the winters for some years in Florida, or rather Edna had and I had flown up and down, and I had always been fond of it, just as I had always had a deep affection for banks and for financial business. A small bank was in fact for sale in the southern state. It would be the kind of business to which I could devote myself in my old age, nothing that would involve me too deeply or energetically, and it would put plenty of distance between me and Toronto, where it was important for my son, Ken, that he should at this time take over command. I decided to have a go at the election, and if that failed, as I rather fancied it would, then I would take a closer look at the Florida situation. If that is how things had gone, it is likely that I would have turned out to be a success as a banker, but it is quite certain that the world would have been a little thinner on the news front. But, in April that year, another letter arrived from Colin Mackinnon, and this one had a complete change of message.

What was happening in Edinburgh is easily explained.

The *Scotsman,* a fine newspaper with great traditions, was going badly to seed. It was surely enough the voice of Scotland but the Scotland of the turn of the century, respected everywhere but living in the past. Its circulation had been dormant for years and its revenues were not keeping pace with its expenses. It had owners who were certainly not thrifty, its operating methods those of half a century earlier. It had been in the ownership of the same family since 1817, when it was founded, and that was a great deal of the trouble. The family had been caught for penal death duties. And I am giving nothing away when I recall that Sir Edmund Findlay was too fond of the national beverage.

.John Noble, who was the Manager, had his hands full. When, at the insistence of the family, he managed to raise another mortgage, he had then to deal with their way of thinking that there was now money in the bank and less need for restraint, when in fact the paper was deeper in debt. The *Scotsman* owned quite a bit of property, shops mostly, on the North Bridge beside its main door and in Market Street below, outside its machine room; these had gained greatly in value and could have been sold to relieve the company of the pressure of its debts, but Noble always suggested that there were difficulties about selling them at a proper price; he knew how the money would have gone, and was protecting his reserve. But by 1953 the debt was so increased that unless something drastic happened the *Scotsman* was doomed. It could only have lasted a few more years or until death duties came to claim it.

This was the verdict that had been given to the partners by James Whitton, an Edinburgh accountant, who had been their financial adviser, had been allowed to go, and then had been recalled in desperation to help them. He had told them bluntly that they had to sell and it was on his advice that Colin Mackinnon had written to me. In that letter Colin asked if I would be interested in buying some shares or just enough to take control, or even one hundred per cent ownership. I replied that I was interested in the purchase of any part or all of the *Scotsman*.

That letter, as may be imagined, threatened to turn my life upside down, but I still had to go on with the election campaign in Canada; if I had dropped out then, leaving the party without a candidate four months before voting day, my name would stink. All I could do to show the *Scotsman* people that I meant business and to find out the financial state of the company, was to send over two of my top executives. That left me talking my way all round the constituency when my thoughts were elsewhere and it seemed a long contest. My recollection is that polling day was on a Monday in August. By the Thursday the democratic processes were completed at York Centre and the following week, Sid Chapman and I flew to Edinburgh. We arrived in the evening and James Whitton and Colin Mackinnon met us at the airport.

Next morning when I went into the negotiating session, I knew that it was not going to be easy to draw back from the opportunity that was being offered. Yet I wondered why they had failed to find a Scots businessman to take it. Was it just shortage of investment capital, or did they have to find a daft Canadian to rise to their bait?

It was an interesting negotiation. In the beginning we were far apart in our ideas of a price that could be called reasonable, but gradually the difference narrowed. James Whitton was supported by Alastair Blair (now Sir Alastair) who was partner in a law firm which acted for Sir Edmund and the Findlays. Whitton was also supported by an old oil-painting behind his desk, a portrait that surely wasn't flattering of John Geoghegan, the former senior partner of the business, of whom he obviously still stood in some awe. During the course of negotiations he kept turning to look at his former master and at last my curiosity got the better of me and I asked him why. He gave a rather sheepish smile.

'Whenever I am doing anything important,' he explained, 'I always turn to look at Mr Geoghegan, almost as if I would catch a hint of approval . . . or otherwise.'

'But you know you won't.'

'Well, he inspires me.'

'Move over,' I said, 'and let me have a look. I'm the one that needs inspiring, not you two.'

When we were just £25,000 apart, I offered to toss for the difference, but Whitton and Blair would not agree. Maybe they felt that it would be a frivolous thing to do in the course of such a serious matter.

But it wasn't only the figures that required agreement. In the first place I had to promise that I would never sell the paper to an Englishman. It was only the fact that I was a Canadian of Scots ancestry that had persuaded the Findlays rather reluctantly to give me the opportunity of dealing with them. As the negotiations proceeded I recalled what James Muir, President of the Royal Bank of Canada at the time, told me on learning of my brash hope of buying the paper: 'I remember the *Scotsman* coming into our home in Peebles when I was young. It ranked next in importance to Holy Writ—sometimes I think it had a slight advantage.'

We had more or less agreed the terms and next morning Alastair Blair announced that he had solved the problem of keeping a partially Scottish control, which was something I didn't know was worrying them. Alastair said he had persuaded two Edinburgh insurance companies to take up the preference shares, to serve, as he put it, as a 'shackle' on me, and if I would accept this the last obstacle was overcome. I laughed at his anxiety. As far as I was concerned, it was flattering that two Scots insurance companies, reputably as incorruptible and as cautious as the Bank of England, should be keen to come into partnership with me. They would be putting up £150,000. I had finally agreed that the Thomson Company of Canada Ltd. in London would pay £393,750 for the 60,000 ordinary shares, which eliminated Sir Edmund Findlay from the Company, but left his brother, Peter, and Australian-born partner, Colin Mackinnon, with 20,000 ordinary shares as well as 100,000 second preference shares of £1. This capitalized the *Scotsman* Publications Ltd., which included the *Edinburgh Evening Dispatch* and the *Weekly Scotsman*, at £775,000, if you valued the 20,000 ordinary shares owned by Peter Findlay and Colin Mackinnon at the price I'd paid for Sir Edmund's.

Now, when I had brought them to the point of signing the agreement, I was the one who hesitated. I left the two of them and Sid Chapman alone with John Geoghegan's portrait, and went for a walk. Hell, I could still say 'No'. As a matter of fact I could say 'No' as well as anybody. Maybe Alastair Blair had been wasting his time getting these dour and cautious insurance men to come in with me.

I think I walked the whole length of Princes Street or at least as far as the Scott monument. Really for the first time I began to have grave doubts about the step I had practically decided to take. But, as I turned back along that historic mile of George Street, which parallels Princes Street and which the Edinburgh people created in the eighteenth century as the centre-piece of their grand new town, I believe that something of the spirit of my enterprising Scots ancestors must have taken hold of me. Those ancestors lived at Westerkirk, Dumfriesshire, and my great-great-grandfather was a very early Canadian settler, having emigrated in 1773. He must have been an adventurous man, and probably a dreamer, too, but I am sure he little thought, as he went, that one of his descendants would retrace his steps two centuries later and assume the control of that pillar of the Scottish establishment, the *Scotsman*.

Somehow the thought of him reassured me. And, feeling again my usual relaxed self, I returned to the accountant's office and, at 59, virtually revoked all my chances of a quiet and leisurely old age.

These had been two hard days of bargaining and Alastair Blair took James Whitton and me over to his house in an elegant street in that 'New' Town not far from Whitton's office in Charlotte Square. He was surprised when I refused his 'dram' and I fancy he was surprised again when, after a while, I said bluntly, 'I like you two guys. You certainly made a good job of this assignment. Now will you both take over my affairs in Edinburgh?' They both agreed they would, and no doubt felt pleased. Neither had the remotest idea of what they were letting themselves in for.

My son, Kenneth, was in London at this time, having a look at the affairs of *Canada Review*, a small magazine I owned there, and he now met me in Glasgow and we went on a ten-day tour of the Highlands and Central Scotland on our way to Edinburgh for the signing of the Scotsman contract on 3rd September.

Before this final signing Ken and I had a long look at the city from the top of a tram, which is no bad way to take stock of a place. From the top of a tram, all of the city's life was spread out before us that day. I remember the tram we took was a No. 14; neither it nor any of the other lines still run. It bumped and rattled us along some famous streets, Princes Street, Leith Walk, down to Pilrig, Newhaven and Granton by the Forth coast, out to Goldenacre and the suburbs beyond. The fare was twopence and I don't know how they managed to make any profit out of that; perhaps they didn't and that's why they had to stop enjoying their trams. Anyway, there, as I say, was all Edinburgh spread out before us as we rattled along; Edinburgh magnificent, classic and beautiful, steeped in history.

I thought of all I had read of Edinburgh's past, of all those remarkable characters who had peopled it; kings and nobles, queens, too, often queens, and priests, ambitious men, and ordinary folk longing for peace, not knowing whether to use a pen or a knife. History and the sense of time are in the atmosphere of the fine old city, and it was on the top of a No. 14 tram, the day before I got down to the final acceptance of Scotland's national newspaper, that I was first touched by the Edinburgh magic.

You can see in nearly every street signs of the achievements of great adventurers and entrepreneurs of daring and resourcefulness. I knew that I had now been drawn into becoming one of them.

I don't think there can be any harm in telling something of the financial affairs of the *Scotsman* now that so many years have elapsed. They had a very heavy bank loan, and it was this that had been causing James Whitton, as financial adviser, and other responsible executives, continual anxiety. As a matter of fact, when he received my cheque for his shares, Sir Edmund had to send, via James Whitton, a considerable sum to the *Scotsman*, money he personally had borrowed from the firm. Much of this had been to pay death duties on his father's estate, but I don't think we are exaggerating when we say the man was given to extravagance. Now the property which I have mentioned the company owned around North Bridge and up to the High Street was entirely superfluous to the newspaper operations and served no useful purpose at all. I quickly decided that the firm's loan to the bank should be eliminated by selling the shops one by one. At the time, I remember, this move was not well regarded in the city and there was a good deal of criticism, but it was the completely proper thing to do. As a matter of fact, not long afterwards I sold the rest of the property to liquidate the second preference shares which the partners, Peter Findlay and Colin Mackinnon held, and I also purchased from them their ordinary shares.

I tried to show Edinburgh that I was being fair in this matter. I remember that after one shoe company had bought one shop I got a very good offer from the Saxone Shoe Co. for adjoining premises. There was nothing in the contracts which said that this could not be done, and as a matter of fact sometimes two or even three shops of the same kind in proximity to one another generate more trade, as a grouping of restaurants will, but I insisted that the first shoe company should be called up and asked whether they would or would not like rivals coming next to them. When they said they wouldn't like it, I told my people to cancel the £60,000 deal.

I had to get the family out of the business. By this time I had James Coltart with me as Managing Director, and Findlay and Mackinnon were impeding what he and I were trying to do, not of course deliberately, but because they could not alter their ways of working. These were still very much of the old days, when it was a family business and when Sir Edmund was an M.P. and often away in Westminster for long spells and his young partners were usually advised by him to leave executive matters to the Manager. I think when we tackled them they were both glad to go, although Colin Mackinnon's wife came to see us and gave Jim Coltart a piece of her mind.

In all only fourteen people were made redundant when we took over. Ian Munro, who became Company Secretary after John Noble went, always insisted that we had very rightly parted company with some people who should have departed years before and he felt sure that no one who knew anything about the business could have blamed me, as some people in Edinburgh certainly did. Later on we also had to cut down on the number of secretaries—there were at least twenty-three we didn't need. This caused a bit of a stir, for it had to happen when Christmas was approaching. But the people who started to wag their tongues about it didn't seem to learn that I gave each girl three months' pay and told her that if she still didn't have a job after that time, she should come and see me personally.

Besides being misrepresented or misunderstood, I made many mistakes, very often in silly small things, and got myself talked about adversely in the closed circles of conservative Edinburgh society. As an example, which you may think absurd (as I did at the time) I remember Ian Munro, the typical Edinburgh accountant, whom I had asked to keep me right about local attitudes and customs, came to me, rather shame-faced, saying that if I decided to change my attire it would be better not to wear my bright blue suit, red tie, red socks and brown shoes. These were Canadian clothes, these were the things I'd been wearing when I went into the composing room to talk to and meet the compositors, intending if I could to impress them with my forthrightness and lack of 'side', and they'd looked down their noses at me, although I was no doubt the only one who could save their jobs for them. I was also advised to buy an old Daimler rather than go about in the Cadillac which had been sent to me across the Atlantic.

Dutifully I did this, but then I very soon learned what the office people were saying as I went by: 'There goes the Chairman in his hearse.' So I bought a new Cadillac in London and the Daimler sure enough did end its dignified days working for a local funeral undertaker.

I was still irrepressibly brash and I couldn't help pulling the legs of the Edinburgh society people when I

16

saw them turning up their noses at me. I remember one occasion when I was a guest at dinner in the Banqueting Hall of the Castle. I was sitting next to Sir Colin Barber, who was Chief of Scottish Command, a man about six feet eight inches tall, known affectionately as 'Tiny' Barber. Sir Colin probably had no idea that he appeared to be representing the old brigade when he asked me, with great gravity, what changes I intended to make in the paper. With a straight face I told him that I was considering putting in a full page of comic strips. The stricken look that came into his face was very expressive. As we were talking between courses, the piper came in, piping and marching round the table. This happened several times and finally I leaned across to Sir Colin and asked, 'Have we got to put up with this?' And he, getting beyond the point of control, demanded, 'What the hell kind of Scotsman are you?'

I also got the reputation for thrift although it was generally given a less friendly name. This thrift, of course, was essential if the *Scotsman* enterprise was going to be run at a profit instead of a loss; to turn an ailing pair of papers—for the *Evening Dispatch* was also running firmly in the red—into a healthy undertaking was going to take all the financial acumen we could muster. When I emigrated to Scotland at the beginning of 1954 my Canadian concerns were making me roughly half a million dollars a year, after tax, which had been more than I could spend, but there had always been some bank loan somewhere to be paid off, there always was if the business was being expanded properly, I reckoned. But I had no intention of siphoning off any more Canadian money into that remarkable edifice towering over Waverley Station in Edinburgh. I wasn't so sure I was going to make a roaring success of it. All I wanted, in fact, was that I could stem the drain of continuing losses. I hadn't taken it on as a money-maker. If I could get it into a solvent state, that would be nice work for what I then called my old age. And obviously the first and vital obligation was to keep the tightest possible rein on expenses until we could put up the revenue. I remember one day I had just been arguing with the *Evening Dispatch* editor about what I considered an extravagance, when five minutes later I was showing a Canadian visitor round the plant and offices. We were in the editorial department when he happened to ask me if it was true that Scots people were as tight as they were reputed to be. 'Not at all,' I said, and glanced across to where, within earshot, the editor of the *Dispatch* was standing. 'I'm tighter than any Scot I've met so far.'

It cost me a lot of good money to part company with the *Dispatch*'s editor, by the way, so maybe he had the last laugh. He would be the first to admit that bringing him to Edinburgh, which was not his style at all, was one of the mistakes I made at the start, and it affected my relations with the city, for if I say that he wasn't nearly so well suited to Edinburgh as I was, I am not exaggerating.

Those who preceded me as owners and operators of the *Scotsman* were a dour and proud lot. In the entrance hall there was a large and florid portrait of James Law by Orpen. He was Colin Mackinnon's grandfather and was business manager of the *Scotsman* for sixty-five years, until he died in 1922. His appearance was stern and his visage forbidding in the picture and every time I passed him he seemed to be giving me warning of the awful fate that would befall me if I went on departing from the traditional ways which he had established.

The *Scotsman* building must have seemed magnificent when it was erected; it was a stone and marble edifice, more suited, perhaps, for the head office of a bank than for the irreverent activities of newspaper production. It had been built on the edge of the cliff above which old

Edinburgh and the Castle are silhouetted against the evening sky. Its main entrance is on North Bridge, from which the building rises for six storeys, but from which it also descends down the face of the cliff to Market Street by the side of the station and the railway. It is then eleven storeys from ground floor to attic, and there was no elevator in it. The building had been erected during the reign of James Law; in the previous office everyone had had to walk up and down the stairs, and he could see no good reason, other than twentieth-century sloth, why they should not continue so to walk in the new building. For some years, when he was already getting on in life, James Law did walk up and down those terrible stairs. But there came a time when, having descended to the Market Street door, he used to take a stroll outside and catch a tram which took him via Princes Street up the North Bridge to his front door half-way up the building.

There was plenty of room in the building for an elevator and that was one of the first things we installed when the hard economy drive could be relaxed a little.

In the interim, I felt sometimes that I was surrounded by enemies; enemies within the gates, so to speak. The editor of the *Scotsman*, Murray Watson, was frankly hostile to me. He appeared to be sure that I would ruin the paper, given the chance, and he waited for me to make one false move that could oblige him to resign in protest, confident that public opinion would be with him, perhaps even to such an extent that I would be forced out of the paper. He was not alone in this attitude, and either it was deliberate or it was a kind of reflex action of people who could not accept that the Findlays had really asked to be 'bought out'. Both in editorial and in management it was easy to sense the antagonism just when we needed to pool all our energies to save the paper. Not too many of the public were on my side either. They resented something they feared rather than anything I actually did; for I had realized very soon after taking over that I had to tread warily. I never gave orders, editorially; just suggestions, which were generally ignored. From every quarter I was warned what would happen to the circulation of the paper if any 'ill-considered' changes took place in it. You would have thought they were talking about a paper that was highly successful.

I began to wonder if I should have bought that bank in Florida instead of immuring myself there in the marble halls of the *Scotsman* on the heights above the statue of Sir Walter Scott where he sat like Lincoln in Washington in his monument.

I never really despaired. The test was going to be who among them and how many among them were going to pitch in and help me when I finally gauged it was time to start modernizing the paper and thumbing my nose to Edinburgh's kirk elders. I could put that off for a certain time, since no one wanted the Canadian stranger to start throwing his weight about, and I could hope that they would begin to appreciate my dilemma. But in the meantime the money was still draining away. I had to be careful not to frighten off those Edinburgh advertisers with their old-fashioned outlook and their antipathy to strangers, especially those wearing red socks, but somehow I had to get more revenue and soon. I had to correct antiquated attitudes in the *Scotsman* (and its Editor) to make it the great paper it once was, and that was going to cost money.

Incidentally when I made James Muir, head of the Royal Bank of Canada, a director of the *Scotsman*, he said he was more proud of that appointment than of any other. It was a terrible blow to me a few years later when he died on a holiday visit to his birthplace, Peebles, a day after he had lunched in London with me and my new colleagues, who were also his colleagues as he had joined the board of the organisation only four months previously. He had shown faith in me in the Forties in advancing money when my first bank thought I was expanding too rapidly, and he gave me a friendship which was irreplaceable.

But in 1954 I saw that the *Scotsman* problem was going to be a trial of will between me and the local people. Much more was at stake than the profit or loss on the £393,750 I had borrowed in Canada to invest in Edinburgh. James Muir, for one, and one or two in the Thomson Canadian offices, and young Ken Thomson, don't forget, were going to look askance at me if I went home defeated in my foray in the old country. I hadn't thought of that when I left, but that was something I couldn't face.

2

GREAT SCOTS AND DOUR SCOTS

MURRAY WATSON, the editor of the *Scotsman*, was a tough character. He never seemed to lose the strength of his determination to resist anything I might suggest, although in fact I never tried to impose any change upon him. It was an obvious necessity that the deadly uninteresting want-ads should be taken off the front page and in their place should be put the thing people should not have to hunt for in a newspaper—news. But it was also apparent to me that such a move ordered by me was just the signal Murray was waiting for.

Those who worked for the *Scotsman* were pretty solidly opposed to the change, and, so far as I could determine, so were the public. Warnings as to the consequences came to me from every side, the reasons given ranging from the ridiculous to the absurd. One man solemnly gave me as his reason the fact that when he picked up the paper from his doorstep on a rainy morning the front page was wet and difficult to read so it was better to have the small ads on the front page! Many made the unqualified assertion that if I put news on the front page they would stop taking the paper.

It was, of course, in those days a slightly revolutionary change to propose. The popular papers had their big headlined front pages to serve as a warning to editors 'of a more responsible kind' and *The Times* had not yet dreamed of such a step, as far as I knew. But I reckoned we needed it as a morale-booster and an earnest of our arrival in the twentieth century, to convince the younger generation, not to speak of the younger advertising men, that there was fresh blood in the old *Scotsman*.

Fate eventually resolved my struggle with Murray Watson. He became ill and had to retire. We bade the old warrior goodbye and started to plan the changes. In fact it took me three years from the time I joined the paper to take the *Scotsman* out of its Edwardian cocoon.

As I grew older I had developed a certain shrewdness that still, I believe, stands me in good stead. It certainly did in this case. What I did was to go to London and hire the Festival Hall, and arrange there a first-class luncheon. To this I invited all the prominent Scots in London, and there are always plenty there heading British business. The guests were greeted by bonny Scots lassies, all with good Scots accents and sprigs of heather for the guests and good legs for the kilts they wore. The food was excellent and the wine flowed freely. I then got up and explained that, as they all knew, the *Scotsman* was a great newspaper and the true voice of their native land, but that it was not enough that Scotland's voice should be heard in Scotland. The time had come when the voice of Scotland should be heard all over the world. Fine patriotic stuff. I now proposed, I said, to carry out a great development of Scotland's national newspaper.

We would promote its sale all over the world. It would go into every embassy and consulate. Everywhere Scotland's voice would be heard uttering the opinions that the country wanted to push and ringing with pride in the country's achievements. 'But,' I said, without blushing, 'we must make fundamental changes in the paper in order to achieve this. We can't send the *Scotsman* into foreign lands with Edinburgh small ads on

B   23

its front page. Foreign countries must see that Scotland is as modern and progressive as any other small country. So, for a start, we will have to put news on the *Scotsman*'s front page.'

The time had come when we all had to sacrifice custom and tradition to project our country into the marketplace of the world. That was the ice broken. Similar lunches followed in Scotland. You might think that we were going to a great length and expense just to get news on to the front page. But, in fact, we were doing more than just softening the blow of the change we were making. We were making the most of the change and the *Scotsman* was gaining from it rather than losing its old readers and friends as people had predicted.

Public luncheons did not so easily or so quickly help us to solve the financial problem, which was a simple matter of building up the volume or the price of advertising, in fact both, to the level when that revenue would begin to carry the *Scotsman*'s production costs, and indeed until we could safely increase these latter outlays. I think that Edinburgh people may well be the least given of all the people of Britain to advertising themselves or their produce and output. They sometimes seem to have a guilt complex, no doubt inherent in them since John Knox's day, which makes them feel that it is wrong to incite others to spend money, unless it is to invest it or tie it up in insurance, of which of course they sell a great deal. But you get this attitude from high and from low. One day I walked out of the office and along the North Bridge I went into a fruit store and told the sales-girl: 'Those are nice-looking grapes. I'll take two pounds.' She looked at me doubtfully: 'They're four shillings a p-pound.' She was trying to protect me against my rashness. South of the Border, I dare say the grapes would have been thrust into a bag and the bag in my hand before I could change my mind.

Progress with the *Scotsman* revenue was slow, but progress we did. It even seemed, perhaps because of the arrival of a new Scottish managing director, that we were attracting less resentment from Edinburgh people.

Jim Coltart did not join me until 1955. My first general manager was Ray Barford from Vancouver, a clever publisher who, I hoped, would apply his expertise successfully into modernizing the *Scotsman*, but who proved to be incompatible with Scottish ways and to Edinburgh especially, and was thankful to get out. I had met Jim when he was host at my table at an international press-conference dinner in Glasgow in 1949, and St. Clair McCabe, my Canadian vice-president, had seen him in the Beaverbrook office in Glasgow, where he managed the *Evening Citizen*, and had been impressed with his knowledge of newspaper economics and administration. St. Clair had told me, 'That's the man who could make a go of the *Scotsman*.'

In the autumn of 1954 we had made a big drive to boost the sale of the *Evening Dispatch*. But the editor we had got from Fleet Street, Jack Miller, who I would say was a smart man in the wrong place, did not seem able to produce the kind of paper that appealed to Edinburgh people. At that time, Jim Coltart had phoned me from the *Citizen* office in Glasgow, asking how long we were going to keep up this circulation war, which affected his paper as our areas overlapped. Jim's call couldn't have been better timed. I took him to dinner at the North British Hotel to sound him out, and afterwards we walked across the North Bridge to the office, where Ian Munro was waiting.

We knew that we needn't try to bluff Jim Coltart, even if we had wanted to, nor to make a half-hearted offer. After the abortive effort to push the *Dispatch* on to a really competitive run against his *Citizen*, he must have been a bit doubtful about our prospects generally to be all that eager to join us. To convince him that he should, we showed him balance sheets and bank statements. But the trump card was the offer that I then made—the general managership of the whole company. It was a big offer for a man who was still comparatively young. But he was not too young to accept it without some negotiation. He said he didn't like the title, which was the Canadian style, and would prefer to be Managing Director. Didn't we want him on the board? He also wanted some assurance about the policy being applied to the *Scotsman*.

I asked him what he was referring to, specifically. Surely he wasn't another of them!

'It's been allowed to slip,' Jim said. 'A few years ago it was still a great national newspaper. It could be again.'

I told him there was nothing I wanted more and that I had a million dollars to back him, if they were needed.

But what really drew Jim Coltart to hitch his wagon to this star was his burning desire at that time to find something that would interest and absorb his invalid wife. He knew that all their married life she had longed to live in Edinburgh. He went back home and told her of my offer and he carried her from the bed in which she had lain for six months and put her, propped up on pillows and wrapped in blankets, into the back seat of the car, and drove her to Edinburgh that night—just to look at the *Scotsman* office. Though it was not to be admitted, maybe he was a little excited himself.

She was happy and she was exhilarated and it was she who was calling the tune. Though he realized that by the time he was installed in the North Bridge office she might be dead, or too ill to be shifted, he wanted to give her this move to think and plan and dream about. She was dying of cancer—in fact she died in February of that year of 1955 without ever having seen Edinburgh after that night—and it was this private gnawing grief of his, and the way he never mentioned it, that drew me strongly to Jim Coltart in those days. I still hadn't got over my time with my wife suffering the same kind of illness.

But we shared a great deal more than a knowledge of what such an illness and bereavement means. You might say we were temperamentally akin. Jim was, and is, a warm character, as genial as I believe I am, and as confident and ready to be tough and aggressive in his business dealings when it became necessary. He was also frank, which I liked. I recall that I quizzed him towards the end of that meeting in the North Bridge office as to why it was taking him so long to make up his mind, when it was obvious he wouldn't refuse the offer of such a top job, and he replied:

'The nearer you are to Roy Thomson, the nearer you are to the door. At least, that's what they say.'

'That's baloney.'

'You did a lot of firing when you arrived here—and had to reinstate some of them.'

'You afraid you'll be fired?' I countered.

Perhaps the thing that drew us swiftly together was the liking we shared for working out in our heads complicated percentages, depreciations, profits and losses, and we both had an aptitude for this work, which made some of our conversations highly mathematical. We were, too, both men who liked power but had no time for pomposity or pretence. There was an aura of 'class' and dignity which permeated the whole office and we went about, each in his own way, purging it of this. We had to deal with our fair share of pompous people and in so doing we had a lot of laughs together. Typically we not only installed a life-saving elevator but we brought the marble staircase into use. This splendid piece of marble leading from the oak-panelled corridor in which Sir Edmund had had his room to the main hall had been reckoned so valuable that it had been put out of bounds to

the staff and used only on state visits and tours of direc-
torial inspection. I couldn't sell it, so it was better used
even if it wore.

Jim Coltart became and remained my closest colleague
during most of these exciting twenty years in Britain.
There had been so much to do, so many mistakes to make
and correct, so much novelty for me in the Edinburgh
life, that I hadn't had time to realize how lonely I was. It
was a real pleasure to have again a colleague I could talk
to, not only in complete confidence but in full understanding, one who understood what I was doing and
why, which I hadn't had since the rupture with Jack Kent
Cooke, and which I certainly needed there in Edinburgh,
more than I had ever needed.

It was Jim who brought in Alastair Dunnett as editor
of the *Scotsman*, when the implacable Murray Watson
was forced by illness to retire. When I learned that he
was thinking of approaching Alastair, I told him that it
was no use, I had already talked to him and the offer was
declined. Jim, however, persisted and the offer was
reconsidered and finally accepted. I don't know how Jim
succeeded in persuading him, but he was able to recall
how often his wife, Margaret, had spoken of Alastair and
once she mentioned how Alastair had confessed to her
that the only thing he could do to help his shy but artistic
wife was to keep her company in the country while she
painted. Before she died, Margaret Coltart had told Jim,
'I can picture you and Alastair working together on the
Scotsman. One day you'll get him to join you and you'll
make a good team.' All this Jim told Alastair, and went
on to talk about the ambitions for the *Scotsman* that were
stirring behind the rather unpopular noises and moves
that I had been making.

A. M. Dunnett was already an experienced newspaper
editor. He was a poet. He had a profound love of his
native country, its traditions and its past. He also knew

the ins and outs of the politics of the present perhaps as well as anyone, for he had been personal assistant to the greatest Secretary of State Scotland had ever had, Tom Johnston.

Alastair was to edit the *Scotsman* with great distinction until 1972 when, as I will relate in another chapter, I became an oil man and persuaded him to become chairman of Thomson Scottish Petroleum Ltd. With Alastair in the editor's room in that sombre panelled corridor, and with Jim as chief executive of the company, the fortunes of the *Scotsman* were at last set fair, and I was happy.

There is no doubt about it I had to take a great many knocks in that city which I grew so much to love. I laid myself out from the start to be friendly, but the doors of all but one of the fashionable houses remained closed to me. The hostility and cold shouldering of the locals would have driven away many a man who might not have been able to turn, as I would have been, to such a rich and assured alternative life. But I had had to keep my head down and my chin in through many years of the icy blast of adversity in northern Canada, fighting for long years to make a little wealth for myself, struggling mostly to pay off my debts, and after all that I wasn't inclined to let Edinburgh lick me.

Alastair realized very quickly, I think, that it would not do the *Scotsman* any harm if he succeeded in acquiring a better public image for its proprietor. For my part, I made it plain that I welcomed his advice and that I wanted to win the respect of the people who mattered in Edinburgh. Alastair brought the Rev. Selby Wright to see me and we carried out a plan about Panmure House, a disused historic dwelling house in the High Street area, in which Adam Smith had lived and which belonged to the *Scotsman*; we restored it and handed it over to Selby Wright as a much needed boys' club. That was a start.

Later we went down together to Westerkirk in Dumfries-shire and Alastair showed me the kirkyard in which was the grave of an eighteenth-century ancestor of mine, and we took a picture of his great-grandson's grandson sitting on the parapet of the bridge his ancestor built so long ago. I was also inveigled into meeting the minister of the kirk and before I quite realized what was happening I was presenting to the church a new pipe organ, which cost a pretty penny, but was duly consecrated in my presence, a memorial to my great-great-great-grandfather who left these parts for Canada. These proceedings must have been a considerable surprise to him, if he was able to observe them from that other place, all happening in the little kirk where, in his youth, he had no doubt lamented the abominably long sermons he had had to endure.

Besides these benefactions, there was £25,000 to the University of Edinburgh; £5,000 each year to the Edinburgh Festival; and prompt support for such schemes as the erection of a memorial on the site of the battlefield at Bannockburn.

One thing I refused to do, when I was seeking to win the respect of the Edinburgh worthies, was to try to change the image of myself that I presented to the world. This I wouldn't do for anyone, though a few good women have tried to persuade me to some change. I think that it is plain to all who know me that I am a simple man. It may not be appreciated that that isn't, and rarely is, accidental. It is my belief, you might call it my philosophy, that in this life you don't achieve simplicity, or preserve it when you are fortunate enough to acquire it, unless you deliberately bar from your way of life, your every-day existence, anything that is phoney. I liked a simple life, I had no pretensions and I didn't want to fool anybody. I liked to be frank and I had got far enough in my life to feel that I didn't need to pretend that I was other than I was.

I'm inclined to blurt things out, and I've had to suffer for some of the things I've said without forethought. Even in business deals I'm rather prone to frankness. I can say at the end of the day that I have never lied to deceive people in business. I don't think it can be said that I have ever gypped anyone. Of course I didn't want to throw money away when I was negotiating for a newspaper, but my philosophy has always been that people should not regret dealing with me, and this in fact has paid off.

During this period in Edinburgh I gained strength from three other sources. One, above all, was Canada, where the change I had effected in the business before I left was apparently working well. Kenneth, my son, had taken over as president. In January they had bought four Florida newspapers and in February the *Nanaimo Daily Free Press* and then in Prince Edward Island the *Guardian*. This was immensely comforting to me as a father, and also, I must confess, flattering to my pride as a Canadian, or, if you like, to the vanity of a man when he reaches his sixties, even if he hasn't had any previously. I felt confident that when I paid my next visit to Canada, in April, to hand over the presidency of Canadian Press, my one-time reputation as owner of obscure country newspapers whose importance was negligible would be no longer adequate cause for a sneer, thanks to my son. We didn't want any fuss made of us, neither Ken nor I, but it was satisfying to realize that we couldn't be ignored either in Canada or the United States, even if Edinburgh noses were still being looked down.

One man who did much to reconcile me to Edinburgh was Teddy Stevenson—Sir Edward Stevenson, Purse Bearer to the General Assembly and to the Lord High Commissioner. Teddy's duties, which included the introduction of guests in the Throne Room at Holyrood House

31

each year, gave him a position of some influence, and he was by way of being a leader of Scottish society, besides being a very likeable chap in his own right. It was James Whitton, the accountant who had negotiated the *Scotsman* deal, who introduced Teddy to me, no doubt surmising that if Teddy could help with my education and with social contacts it wasn't impossible that I might give *him* some advice on financial matters, which from all accounts he needed. It was difficult for anyone not to like Teddy instantly, and in fact we became, during the next year or two, such good friends that he and his wife came to stay with me in Canada for a holiday and were taken everywhere from Niagara to Timmins. It was a very sad blow indeed to me when he died, suddenly and prematurely, at the end of 1957.

The third source of comfort and strength which sustained me at this time was my own home. When I first arrived in the city I stayed in Sir Edmund Findlay's old house in Rosebank while the villa I had bought in the Braid Hills district was got ready. A woman interior decorator had been commissioned to decorate and furnish the house. I've never hesitated to pay for expertise and this was a house that deserved to be maintained with skill and taste. It had belonged to Sir James Learmouth, surgeon to George VI. But I had a disagreement with this young woman over the choice of curtains and carpets. With my daughter Irma's help I got the house looking beautiful according to my own notions, so decorated and furnished, you might say, that it never drove me out in the evenings to seek relaxation elsewhere, as perhaps it might have done. The heating was installed under the directions of 'Wullie' McMunagle, works manager of the *Scotsman*, whose pride in doing the job was worth seeing, although as a good spartan Scot he was aghast at my demand for a constant 70 degrees. He also did a good job bidding for and picking up for me pieces I had marked in the auctioneers' catalogues. Attending the sale-rooms was practically the only pleasure for which I took time off. Long after the house was well furnished I was still going to see items of silver, which I had collected for years and in which Dowell's Edinburgh sale-rooms excel. The sale-room staff also excelled in spotting Roy Thomson bidding from the back of the crowd, so I had more often than not to send 'Wullie' in my stead. I also began or developed an extensive collection of antique rings—I've got over three hundred now—and somewhat embarrassed my secretary, Miss Gladstone-Miller, by asking her to try on the first new purchase when I got back to the office. Don't ask me why I took a particular interest in rings; they were and are beautiful, and, of course, they have appreciated enormously in value.

Wullie McMunagle, incidentally, was a little annoyed when, having given a good deal of his own time to attending sales for me, something small for himself was inadvertently included on my account and he was later asked for his cheque by my very efficient secretary. It was for two guineas and might, he felt, have been overlooked. Some time later he took his revenge when I came home from Japan with a new fountain pen, purporting to be a Schaeffer. Something had gone wrong with it and I asked Wullie if he could get it fixed. He returned next day looking very smug indeed and informed me with relish that I had been done, the pen was a fake and the repair which he had had carried out would cost me two guineas. I paid up without a murmur.

I left Wullie, as I have said, to see to the heating in my house, merely stipulating that he should ensure for me an even temperature of 70 degrees from front door to back and cellar to attic. This he did with typical Scottish thoroughness and in time it had a curious effect upon the house; the fine oak doors and other woodwork had become seasoned to the kind of cold that the Scots seem masochistically to enjoy in their homes, or used to. My continuous 70 degrees caused warping and cracks, which caused Wullie to stop chuckling over the boss's Japanese pen.

The pleasure I had in my home, however, derived not so much from its mechanical fittings and its contents as from the couple who looked after its comforts and mine, a German couple, Gunther and Hanni Hirsch, who are still with me and whose thoughtful attention to my needs has immured me from all adversities, disappointments and frustrations. When I was driven home by Gunther, I could shut that stout oaken door behind me, look at my Gainsborough on the staircase and the Raeburn on the landing, feel the warmth of those spacious bright rooms with their big overstuffed armchairs, eat one of Hanni's wonderful meals, play a little with my dog, Whitey, whose devotion was never in question, and read a balance sheet or a who-dunnit. Once inside that front door, it was easy to forget Edinburgh's grudging behaviour.

It took us, in fact, ten years less a few months to solve the financial problems of the *Scotsman*. This is not to say that it did not in itself become a viable paper before that. But it is not, and I don't think ever will be, a big profit-maker, nor does anyone expect that of such a paper. Certainly I don't. You may remember that I came to Edinburgh and became involved with the *Scotsman* and its problem (which was in the first place a problem of survival) not as a philanthropist but with a view to having something I could enjoy doing in my old age, while Ken carried on the money-making concern we had in Canada; that was a small shoe-string operation compared with the £300m. Thomson companies of Canada of today. We had then some sixteen small-town news-papers and three small radio stations, but the company was on the way up under my son's chairmanship and the skilful management of St. Clair McCabe and Sid Chapman. The business in Canada was already earning enough to satisfy all the pecuniary needs of myself and my son. I wasn't looking for any substantial addition to that from the Edinburgh undertaking.

But I was determined not to take any additional money out of Canada to sink and lose in the *Scotsman* company, and in my experience nothing can lose money with such an air of success as a British newspaper. So I wasn't going to leave it alone; there was no question of retiring until I had got it into good enough financial shape to leave to my son. That was the challenge. There was also the small matter of demonstrating to the Edinburgh people how wrong they had been in looking down their noses at the contribution I was making, or proposed now to make, to the history of their city.

The real trouble with the *Scotsman* was that it was tied to the *Evening Dispatch*. With my knowledge of Canadian newspaper economics, I saw from the start that the situation could contain a nice drain for any mug's money. A city of half a million people like Edinburgh could not support two evening papers as well as a daily that took a big share of the local advertising. The Edinburgh people, and I mean the Edinburgh business people, were a somewhat proud community that was probably the least given to advertising in the Western world. That lack of advertising, however much you wrung out of the big stores, the churches, schools, local government, banks and insurance companies, could not be set aside whatever the success with the circulation. What we needed was a sensible application of the one-paper solution which we had worked very generally in Canada and the United States.

A community of a certain size could only support one newspaper and that was almost always an evening paper. Readers grabbed a national daily like the *Scotsman* when they were breakfasting or commuting or if they were housewives enjoying a mid-morning break, but in their leisure time they wanted to turn from national to more local news and to local classified ads as provided by the evening paper. In Edinburgh as in Winnipeg.

In Canada and the United States we now own newspapers in 103 towns. Only three of these towns have a morning paper. None has two evenings. Because our operations (like other newspaper companies') restricted these communities to the service of only one newspaper, it did not mean that these communities suffered. Two rival newspapers, each struggling to make ends meet and dragging out any old scandal that they think may sell a few copies, aren't performing the service that one prosperous and healthy newspaper could. You see them doing everything they can to please their advertisers (even suppressing news, maybe). Often they cannot afford to maintain a good news service, or the number of pages on which to print it, because of the cost of newsprint, and local people have to buy both papers to catch all the news or to see all the advertised opportunities and coming events. Many advertisers, on the other hand, feel they have to go into both papers. When a single newspaper takes over in that situation it does not necessarily charge double for advertising, but it can, at least, safely raise the rate to cover its newsprint, news-getting and production costs.

This, of course, was what we had to do in Edinburgh. But the *Evening Dispatch* was, in my opinion, a better paper than the *Evening News*, its rival. It had the advantage of coming out of a stable which had a morning paper to back it and share some of the costs. It ought to lick the *News*, I thought. The *News* didn't really worry. It had a much stronger circulation and it had almost a monopoly of the small ads. The *News*, by tradition and habit, was the evening paper for the home delivery, for the family. Moreover, in the outlying areas, in Fife and in Stirlingshire, where we might have hoped to be able to expand, we encountered fierce competition from the Glasgow and Dundee papers.

For a long time I felt that I would not yield; I wanted to beat the *News* in a straight fight. I fancied I had the nerve and the resilience; and I didn't have shareholders to worry about. After the rather disastrous period when the *Dispatch* was losing circulation fast, we began to think we would have to negotiate a settlement. In the meantime we let our rivals know that we had plenty of money and that we were going to continue spending it until we had made a success of the *Dispatch*. When, for example, the *News* had a word with Jim Coltart about putting the price of the paper up, they were given the dry message that the *Dispatch* had no intention of joining in this rise, the *News* could do what they liked but we would remain at 2*d*. This, I hoped, would give them further evidence that I was mad, and that there was no ordinary chance of getting me to admit defeat.

In fact it took in all ten years. That was also because the *News* belonged to United Newspapers which had been built up by Sir Harley Drayton, whose money-making activities were extensive enough to relieve him of any worries about the relatively small profit we were allowing the *News* to make. Since all our efforts couldn't turn that profit into a loss, and since the *Dispatch*'s loss was approaching £350,000 a year, while the *Scotsman* profit was around £75,000, it was my move. By this time, of course, we were a very much bigger concern, as you will see, and we were not being driven into a corner.

Harley Drayton came to see me in my office, but there was no urgency in his case, either. He didn't like leaving an unhealthy situation anywhere when it could be remedied, and he had come to see me with everything worked out.

'Well, Roy, what paper will you give me in exchange for the *Edinburgh Evening News*?'

'Blackburn,' I said at once. I also had done some homework, and I didn't for a moment believe he would accept my offer. He didn't.

'Sheffield,' I said then.

The idea was to surprise him and I think I did. I guessed he had come to ask for Sheffield. It would fit better than the *Edinburgh News* into the territorial spread of his enterprises, his United Newspapers certainly. Sheffield also had a morning paper and the two, morning and evening, were making between them a profit in the region of £400,000, whereas his Edinburgh office was making only about £200,000. He murmured approvingly.

'You'll have to compensate me for loss of earnings,' I said.

The surprises, sometimes engineered, in those negotiations have always been for me the spice of life. I waited for his next one.

'Look, Roy,' he said. 'Don't let's bring anyone else into this. We don't need bankers; you and I can work it out quicker and better on our own. Come to my house in Kensington Palace Gardens and we'll finish the deal in no time.'

If he wanted it that way, I said, it would suit me, too. I didn't for a moment have any thoughts about being outmanœuvred because I didn't have Warburg's with me. I knew exactly what Harley Drayton wanted; he believed like me that a good deal was one in which both sides were satisfied. He genuinely preferred to have no one interfering when he and I were working to that end. This is the face of capitalism which is quite genuine.

He was, of course, no more a philanthropist in this matter than I was, but I knew, I had known before we started, that I could get a bargain out of the Edinburgh-

Lord Thomson at home at Alderbourne Arches, Buckinghamshire: 'a happy man'

With his daughter, Mrs E. R. Campbell, and son, Kenneth, after receiving the accolade of G.B.E., Buckingham Palace, February, 1970

On the bridge at Westerkirk, Dumfriesshire, built by his ancestor 1735

A *Sunday Times* dinner to inaugurate the new Post Office tower, Lord Thomson with, on his right, Mr Anthony Wedgwood Benn, then P.M.G., and on his left Sir Christopher Chancellor; facing, Sir Isaac Woolfson and Sir Donald (now Lord) Stokes

At the dinner to honour Lord Beaverbrook on his 85th birthday, Lord Thomson introducing his old friend to the microphone, to make his unforgettable last public speech

Five years later, Lord Beaverbrook's son, Sir Max Aitken welcoming Mr Heath and Lord Thomson to the dinner he gave to honour Lord Thomson on his 75th birthday.

Photo Daily Exp

Sheffield deal. Although there was the difference between the Edinburgh profit of £200,000 and the Sheffield figure of £400,000 to be bridged, there was also the loss on the *Dispatch* to be reckoned. I would be getting rid of that £350,000 loss as well as losing the £200,000 profit margin between Edinburgh and Sheffield, which would put me £150,000 up before we started to talk in money terms. These figures were of course clear to both sides, for we had taken along our balance sheets and bank statements to that elegant house in Kensington. But I also felt that in Sheffield sooner or later I might have had to close down the morning paper, which I would have hated to do (United Newspapers have kept it going, but in the long term it will have as difficult a time to survive as most of the other dozen provincial dailies). I also knew that in Edinburgh, once the *News* was amalgamated with the *Dispatch* and run on a tight rein as I could run it, it would make a great deal more than the £200,000 which was the figure we were negotiating on. In fact its profits in some recent years have been touching £800,000. This is how capitalism, presenting its better face, still makes excellent profits.

That was how we got the *Evening News*, sitting in Harley Drayton's comfortable study in Kensington Palace Gardens, again in a street where history had been busy through the years. It wasn't in my experience the strangest place for making a deal. But it was there, and not until then, that the *Scotsman* was finally saved for posterity.

3

A LICENCE TO PRINT MONEY

CONSIDERING THE money that was very soon to be made in it, it seems strange now that, in all the negotiations for the *Scotsman*, no one appeared to give any thought to the prospect of ITV starting in the north, as it was bound to do, with the likelihood of an opening in it for Scotland's national newspaper. In 1953 plans for Independent stations in London were already well advanced. But, from the start, I was so excited by the prospect of getting control of the *Scotsman*, my first sizeable newspaper, and then having such a struggle to make a go of it, that I had no thoughts for any other affair. The *Scotsman* ownership never allowed me a moment to look around, not, anyway, at the start.

When I got round to thinking of the new TV stations, in October 1954, I had been in Edinburgh all of nine months. After making tactful inquiries, I felt I was encouraged by the Independent Television Authority to tender for the programme contract for the Scottish area. It did not take me long, either, to discover that no one else of any consequence was showing any interest in competing for that franchise. No one else would touch it with a barge-pole, I was told.

This, I felt, was a foolish attitude. True, the London companies were running up heavy losses from the moment they had begun to operate. But this was understandable. Previous to the opening of Independent Television, all the TV sets in the country had only one control which people turned on to get the one (BBC) station. To get ITV they now had to buy a conversion unit to attach to their sets, and many people did not hurry to do this. Consequently advertisers were scarce. In these circumstances the programme companies' approach appeared to me to have been too lavish. They had put everything on a big-money, big-time basis, for which there had never been the kind of revenue that would have kept them out of the red. But television paid good profits in the States and in Canada. There, of course, advertising was much more plentiful, the potential of advertising had been developed far beyond the limits known in old-fashioned Britain. Even in newspapers we had a long way to go here, and with this leeway to be tapped, it didn't seem possible that a television station would possibly fail in the long run.

I hadn't come to Edinburgh looking for such dividends, but now that they were in effect on offer and no one else wanted to risk going for them, how could I refuse the chance? It might, in the meantime, take long enough to make the *Scotsman* company pay, and it might be better to have a second string to my bow. As I had found in Timmins, broadcasting and newspaper business went well together, and strengthened each other.

Something was wrong that I, a Canadian, could come into Scotland and have this opportunity dangled in front of me, and I guessed I had better go about this business with some caution. First, I wanted some good Scots people to form a company with me, if possible leading Scots whose names would be enough to guarantee high principles in our endeavour.

In the first months of 1955 I wrote many letters, and not only to those with money. I was advised in this delicate work by Sir Edward Stevenson, and, his being

a good name for a start, I insisted that he must join the
TV company, and I made sure that the bank would accept
my guarantee for any advance he needed for this purpose.

Starting at the top, I began to write to all the dukes and
lords and heads of clans; I presented my proposition to
law-lords and heads of Scottish businesses; I turned to the
noble chairmen of insurance companies and banks; I came
down the scale to provosts and well-to-do shopkeepers;
and I eventually even approached the Scottish Co-
operative Society and the Labour Party. From high to low
I asked them quite simply for their support and investment in the project of providing Scotland with the best
possible television service. I mentioned that I already
had the backing of Sir Edward Stevenson, Sir Compton
Mackenzie, and James Whitton, who was now on the
board of the *Scotsman* company. 'Monty' Mackenzie,
whom I had met at many functions in Edinburgh, and
who, I fancy, was one of those who induced me to sub-
scribe £5,000 a year to the Edinburgh Festival, had
promised to invest £50 in the TV company; in the
event he made it £40, of which he was only called upon
to put in £16. As the refusals continued, so did my
letters continue to go out. The file of these letters still
exists; it contains the names of the élite of the nation.

Many excuses were offered: other commitments, a
dislike of TV, a conviction that the losses being suffered
by the TV companies in England would certainly be
incurred in Scotland, a willingness but no wherewithal,
'my company would not like my connection with this
enterprise', and so on. No one expressed a reluctance to
go into partnership with Roy Thomson, the barber's son
from Timmins, though no doubt that, also, was a
reason for rejection.

It is ironic now to look at those refusals, to think of the
money those men, some of them shrewd in business and
in affairs, could have made. Among them were Lord

Bilsland, Lord Rosebery, Sir Iain Colquhoun, George Outram and Co. (publishers of the *Glasgow Herald*), Hector McNeil, M.P. (a former Labour Minister), Sir Hugh Fraser, Sir A. B. King (the Glasgow cinema owner who said he did not want to be associated with a failure, which he was sure it would be, but later led the company that obtained the contract for the Aberdeen station), Lord Elgin, the Duke of Hamilton, the Mackintosh of Mackintosh, Sir Harold Yarrow, Admiral Dalrymple-Hamilton, Sir Will Y. Darling (an Edinburgh department-store owner and also M.P. at one time) the Earl of Crawford, Lord Weir, Brendan Bracken and Lord Beaverbrook.

Brendan Bracken begged me to have nothing to do with television and he was horrified that I should be willing to ask the Scottish T.U.C. and the Scottish Co-op. to become shareholders, an invitation which they both rejected. Beaverbrook said, 'I'm a newspaper-man and I'm not interested—and nor should you be.' For once I doubted Max's motives. He had conducted a campaign against commercial television in the *Express*, which was now gloating over the impending bankruptcy of the independent companies, assessing their losses at £5,000 a day. Beaverbrook, I suspect, was caught up in the old fear that TV would take away a damaging slice of the advertising that used to go into newspapers, whereas I reckoned that British newspapers had not skimmed the surface of the country's potential of advertising and there would be plenty for papers *and* TV.

Outram's invited Jim Coltart to discuss my proposition, which was that, if they took a thousand shares, it would greatly help the application for the contract, since there would then be a newspaper from the West of Scotland as well as one from the East concerned in the Company. He promised them that if, at the end of a year,

43

they wanted to back out, then they could depend upon a personal guarantee from me to get their £1,000 refunded. They would, in other words, be coming into the enterprise with no risk to themselves. The Outram's directors asked Jim to step outside while they discussed the proposal and then informed him that they 'did not want to get involved with TV.'

In Scotland, I got my only substantial financial support from the theatre-owning company, Howard and Wyndham, one of whose directors, Charles McQueen, an Edinburgh stockbroker, was a good friend to me in those days and later. I had already begun to look round for premises and Charlie took me to Glasgow to see the Theatre Royal. This looked my best prospect, to convert into offices and studios. Charlie introduced me to Jack Radcliffe and Jimmy Logan, two Glasgow comedians, who, when I told them they could have a slice of Scottish Television and advised them to take it, both put their names down for a thousand pounds, the two comics having more perspicuity than the leaders of the country's commercial world.

Charlie McQueen subscribed £10,000 of his own money (of which £3,824 was called in) and persuaded Howard and Wyndham to put up £40,000 (£16,000 called in). Charlie told me he had wanted them to take STV shares for the £105,000 I was to pay for the theatre. They wouldn't agree and thereby lost a sizeable fortune.

But that is anticipating much that had to be plotted and performed. So far my only real support had come from a theatre company. And almost daily I was dictating the same letter in reply to the refusals that were coming in:

Dear ——,

I have your favour of the ——. I quite understand why you are unable to take part in our new television venture, although I am sure we will have your best wishes. I feel we can do a great service to the country and I am proceeding with the enterprise on that assumption.

Kind regards,

Yours sincerely,

R. H. Thomson.

I was happy to receive a subscription, which was for £1,000, from Lord Balfour of Inchrye; his was a very highly respected Scots name. He brought in later a relative of his, John Profumo, the former Cabinet Minister, for £2,000. And a £200 promise from Lady Mathers was gratifying enough; her husband, a Labour peer, had been Lord High Commissioner to the General Assembly of the Church of Scotland. But I was still counting my team on my fingers. What would the ITA think of my slender support, when I finally put in the application?

None the less, we had to go on with certain preparations as if the contract was already ours, though the ITA went out of its way to warn us, when we notified them of the details that had been settled, that there was still one other applicant in the field.

Already we had been in touch with a top executive of American television, Rai Purdy, and had agreed that, if we got the contract, he would be director of programmes. Meanwhile Jim Coltart, who was going to be Managing Director when the company started operating, went off on a quick tour of television studios in Canada and the States, examining their management techniques and budgeting and hopefully finding ideas that would avert, in Scotland, the disastrous financial losses that were threatening to wreck the English companies. Already we had also prepared estimates of advertising rates; we had research figures for the spending power *per capita* in Scotland as compared with South of the Border. We had

45

found out the cost of post office land-lines. We could make a shrewd guess of how little Manchester or Birmingham or London would take for canned pro- grammes they had already used, and American soap operas, wild westerns and so on, which we believed we could get cheap, since there wasn't another station bidding for them, and if need be we calculated we could fill a lot of hours that way, as I had filled the hours on the air of North Bay with old records.

In response to a questionnaire sent by the ITA, I listed my twenty-four years' experience of radio and the fact that I shared ownership of television stations at Kingston and Peterborough in Canada. I made sure that, if the Authority checked, they would find that I paid British income-tax and that I was legally domiciled in Edinburgh, though still owning a house in Toronto. 'They might turn down my tender,' I wrote to Teddy Stevenson at this time, when I was in Australia at a Commonwealth Press Conference, 'if they question my Scottish residence and rate me a Canadian. If you should be talking to anyone concerned, perhaps you could mention that I am attending this conference as a British delegate and not as a Canadian.'

That letter gives some idea of the political wisdom which I felt at the time had to be employed. As the time of decision grew nearer, I devoted all my day and every day to the project.

It now looked as if, of the £400,000 deemed necessary to start the station, I would have to commit myself to £320,000. This was a big sum to risk. I felt 80% certain that Scottish TV would pay very good profits in the long-run. I had had experience of this kind of situation in Canada and I wasn't frightened by it. Jim Coltart and I could keep the losses to a minimum in a tight situation.

Fortunately I had a third good friend in Edinburgh, Ian Macdonald, who was a near neighbour in the Braid

Hills and, which was rather more important, was General Manager of the National Commercial Bank of Scotland. I had completed all my inquiries at the other TV studios, to see how they got rid of their money, Jim Coltart had studied the workings of the North American companies hurriedly but thoroughly, and I had figured out on innumerable backs of innumerable envelopes just what our estimates must be. With these cut and dried in my mind, I went to see Ian.

Ian Macdonald has played a tremendously important part in my British life. On some counts, you might say I owe more to him than to anyone. It was my luck, too, to meet such a forward-thinking banker practically on my own doorstep. He had been a professor of accountancy and had recently given that up and also his directorship of the Commercial in order to become its General Manager—gleefully, I think, for it is rare for a professor to get into the thick of what he has been teaching, and to be given the opportunity of practising what he has been preaching. And Ian Macdonald's pet thesis was, by happy chance, that there should be an extension of the banks' lending system.

Anyway, there in his house round the corner from mine in Braid Avenue, I told him where I stood, and how I reckoned I could run a TV station more economically than had been done hitherto in England, and how much I needed. He said he had no fear that I would fail and he was prepared to let me run up a debt on my personal account of half a million. He shook his head when I said I could get the loan guaranteed by Canada. He didn't need that.

This was the kind of backing that I badly needed that day to bolster my morale as well as to make sure that I could keep my vow not to go back for more money from Canada. I was now poised for the big gamble.

And sure enough, it had to be at this very moment that

I found I had talked myself into the biggest party I had ever given in Edinburgh. I had visited NATO head-quarters as one of a delegation at the end of 1954, and had met the Supreme NATO Commander in Europe, General Alfred Gruenther. I had secured his presence at a dinner in Edinburgh by the simple expedient of asking him. When officialdom found out that the Supreme Commander was visiting Edinburgh at the invitation of Roy Thomson, things began to move. The guest-list, for instance, had to be extended to include all those whom protocol demands should pay their respects to a Supreme Commander on a public visit to an allied country. Everyone from Lord John Hope, joint Parliamentary Under-Secretary for Foreign Affairs, to Sir John Banks, the Lord Provost, had to be invited. When Gruenther arrived at Turnhouse, he had however to be met and shaken by the hand by me. Cameras clicked and then off he was dragged by officialdom for an official tour, before he was finally delivered up that evening for one of the most brilliant dinners Edinburgh had ever seen, for I may have been a brash Canadian but this was one field of human endeavour in which I was as sophisticated as they come.

It had occurred to me, of course, that the publicity of this visit to Roy Thomson in Edinburgh would not be altogether lost on the ITA. At any rate, I didn't keep out of the way of my own photographers nor the visiting TV men. Perhaps a dinner to General Gruenther couldn't have been better timed.

And finally, on 24th May, the letter arrived. It told us, in the dry way of all such letters, that on the following Wednesday a press conference would be held in the North British Hotel to announce that we had been awarded the Authority's contract to set up a Scottish Television Company, and it urged us to mention this fact of our successful application to no one in the meantime. This last request was the toughest the ITA had made of me. The following Wednesday the press was issued with a hand-out announcing the founding of Scottish Television Limited, under the chairmanship of Roy Thomson. We had no studio, no artists, no announcers, no producers, no technicians, no musicians and no programmes but we had a contract (signed on 19th June, 1957).

I remember that when the letter arrived Jim Coltart was sitting opposite me and I tossed it over to him. He read it.

'What do we do first?' he asked.

'I haven't an idea.'

Jim stared at me for a moment. 'Roy, I get a certain impression that you know nothing about running a TV station.'

'That's quite correct.'

He looked horrified. 'But you said in the application to the Authority that you were part-owner of two stations in Canada!'

'Well, I am. But I only took a share in them to give Rupert Davies—Senator Rupert Davies—some financial backing when he needed it. I've never had anything to do with the running of them.'

Jim Coltart closed his eyes as if to shut out the sight of a cruel world, then broke into a laugh. 'That's fine,' he said. 'So we both begin from scratch.'

Of course I had had a good deal of experience of running commercial radio stations.

There is in the *Scotsman* office in Edinburgh, carefully preserved, the old ruled exercise book which was the first register of shareholders in Scottish Television Ltd. and it may interest you to see the names of the people who came with us in this venture. The figure after each name is the amount they were called upon to contribute, that amount being only two-fifths of what they had committed themselves to pay in if needed. A third of each of

these contributions was for ordinary shares, the rest
being debentures which were very soon paid back, and
it may be of interest that those who then had £100
worth of ordinary shares found these had become worth
£22,000 when we went public. These were the lucky and
the daring ones:

Howard and Wyndham, £16,000
Lord Balfour of Inchrye, £400
Sir Edward Stevenson, £2,400
Charles N. McQueen, £3,824
(Sir) Peter Macdonald, £400
John Stewart Clark, £400
(Sir) Ian M. Stewart, £2,000
Charles A. Neale, £800
Rai Purdy, £400
J. M. Davidson, £400
Lady Mathers, £80
J. M. Coltart, £400
Jack Radcliffe, £400
Sir Compton Mackenzie, £10
Alastair Blair, £80
James Allan Short (Logan), £400
J. H. B. Munro, £80
J. A. Jelly, £400
John Dennis Profumo, £800
Ian W. Macdonald, £320
James Whitton, £400
Thomson British Holdings Ltd., £124,800.

The capitalisation of the whole company was only
£160,000. This sum was the 40 per cent call-up of the
amounts which had been subscribed, the total of sub-
scriptions being £400,000. We took £120,000 of this
£400,000 in the form of debentures which were paid off
by borrowing from the bank within six months. Then
there was £40,000 consisting of £36,000 of ordinary

shares and £4,000 of £1 deferred ordinary voting shares. As I had subscribed 80 per cent of the capital, I kept 80 per cent of these voting shares and spread the rest pro rata among the other subscribers.

In a way the situation was one I had faced before, when opening my first radio station in North Bay. But in Scotland at least we didn't have to get on the air as soon as the wires were connected. We had a year and three months in which to prepare everything. Enough time to make mistakes, I thought, squaring my jaw in a way that I hoped brooked no good to anyone who started to waste our limited substance.

First thing, now as in North Bay, was to secure premises and studio space, so we got in touch with Stewart Cruickshank, who was executive head of Howard and Wyndham, and made an offer for the Theatre Royal. That day in his London office Stewart was sticking at a bottom price of £110,000 and I was defending my top offer of £100,000. Finally I took a penny from my pocket and said to him: 'Stewart, we are good friends. We can't stick on this. Let's toss for it.' He was scandalized and immediately settled for splitting the difference at £105,000.

As Jim and I got into the cab to return to Heathrow after a good morning's work, I took out the penny: 'You've never seen a penny before that was worth £5,000.'

I will never forget how we made the first deal for network programme material. Jim and I met Prince Littler, Val Parnell and Lew Grade in a room at ATV. There we began to haggle over the price STV would have to pay to participate, none of us having an idea of what the amount should be. As we were bandying figures about, Prince Littler would dodge over to the desk every now and then and do some sums on paper. Val did most of the talking and I recall telling him he hadn't a hope of brow-beating me, and there was Lew bringing his nose pretty well up against mine with the index finger of each hand on either side of my face and saying, 'What a Jew! What a Jew!'

When we got the station operating it was apparent that we had made a very reasonable deal. This was very helpful in the early stages of our operation. Certainly, our price was the envy of other stations as they came on the air in later years.

Lew Grade was always behind us. He was a tower of strength in our operation. He is one of the most able, decent and efficient operators I have met. He has given me a genuine friendship and his unselfish and helpful behaviour to me and to STV through the years I can never sufficiently repay.

The conversion of the Theatre Royal was begun in mid-February the following year after the last of Howard and Wyndham's contracted performances, and a suite of offices was created for Jim Coltart and his staff out of the dress circle bar. Jim also remained Managing Director of the *Scotsman* and commuted between Edinburgh and Glasgow, often daily, spending the morning in Edinburgh and being engrossed in the problems of television by evening. The recruiting of staff began, almost none of them having any prior experience of TV. Press photographers learned to work the big cameras, radio mechanics handled the cables, repertory actors announced the news. Our hopes of setting up the studios on economical Canadian lines, by which anyone who was under-employed in one job assisted his mate in another, were speedily dashed. Trade-union officials were early on the scene. Precedents for how many men were required for each job had been agreed with the BBC. They were not going to allow a 'commercial' enterprise to upset that pattern. The upshot was we had ultimately to take on 250 men and women, a number that was soon on the increase, for a station never providing more than twelve hours a week of its own production, an operation in fact smaller than that of Station WTTG in Washington, where the staff employed for years had never been more than 85.

This wanton waste of manpower made me lose my temper. 'It can't take three Britons to do the work of one American,' I raged. I was concerned then about the future of the station. If the advertising situation continued against it, as it had been doing for a heartbreaking two years in the south, it might become impossible, and we would have to close down. Then, I was prepared to bet, the union would not find work for all these men and women to whom they had compelled us to offer a future.

This, as a Canadian, I saw as the British malaise. It was growing up at that time and I believe that it had settled pretty heavily over most of this land of ours. It was best illustrated in every industry by the continuing drive of the unions concerned to keep more men employed in any given company than were really necessary, rather than to strive for higher production and consequently higher pay. The unions knew they were doing this. They were unblushing about it. They seemed to me still to be operating with the spectre of the mass unemployment of the Depression years looming over them. What a tragic mistake they were making! For we had gone a long way since those days and every other country in Europe had gone a long way further than we had, with greater growth in their productivity and in their national wealth and in the standard of living of their citizens. Of course I still had complete faith in the British people, otherwise I would not have invested so much money in this country. But the malaise was still there.

No one, of course, wanted to see these excess employees queueing instead for the dole. But would they? There were many industries and services short of labour;

transport, for instance. The sad thing was, to secure real progressive prosperity in this compact and rich little country, to increase greatly the standard of living of even the poorest, all that was needed was only a tiny step-up in national effort, an almost unnoticeable extra push, or one less restriction, in workshops and factories. But that small increase in production, a matter of 2 per cent, would enormously increase the saleability of many of our goods and would inevitably increase the amount of employment at home, of genuine employment figures.

This was obvious to me; I suspect it was obvious to most people, including most workers. But nobody could move against the vast and unthinking monolith of the trade unions. This grieved me, for I was raised in a country where every man wants to get on and is determined to make more money even if he has to work harder, and you can see this determination everywhere, and God help the union official who tries to interfere.

It was of this I sat thinking glumly in the dark of the Theatre Royal, Glasgow, as we auditioned all sorts of singers, players, laughter-makers. And fortunately for the 250 employees of Scottish Television, the upturn in the economy that London and Birmingham and Manchester had been so desperately waiting for, occurred at the very moment when we in Scotland had our new order books ready to start booking time. One couldn't tell at first that the wind had changed. We had no means of comparison. No one in London or Manchester called on the phone to say, 'Go pick up your cherries, the branches are laden,' for, of course, an upturn is never so emphatic as that, anyway. But, from the start, someone was instructed to bring me a carbon of every order for advertising time on Scottish TV and I used to carry these folded in a deep poacher's pocket in my coat, and referred to them repeatedly whenever I was having a cup of tea round the corner. I always knew the running total of income and I could go into the accountant's office and get a fair idea of how much had been spent. I always knew where we stood before anyone else did. And I very soon sensed that the lean years of television were over.

There was still need for great caution. We learned later that TV finances withered or bloomed according to the Chancellor's demeanour. In a cautious financial situation, however, I am in my natural element. It isn't meanness, though some people are happy to call it that. I hate waste, that is all. I never saw any sense in building luxurious offices as they did in England. And I remember how Lewis Hynd, my chief accountant and company secretary, produced his first budget. He had been working over it for weeks, taking it home with him as if afraid to leave it, and paring away at every item. They had made a room for me high above the old stage, and there he came to me and laid the budget in front of me. I had, in fact, already figured how little we could spend. I turned to Lewis. 'Have you gone out of your mind?' I asked. 'We're not spending half that money!'

I recall, too, when STV had gone on the air, I found we had a small ensemble performing every day in a lunch-time programme for which the advertising figures were not particularly high. I got hold of Rai Purdy, who was director of programmes, and told him he was making the same mistake as the TV companies had made in London. They were starting off to beat the daylights out of the BBC in Scotland in the first week, before they could even reckon what the revenue was. I pointed out to him that there were five men in that ensemble; why didn't he hire a Wurlitzer organ, which would save four fees each day? People eating their lunch at home wouldn't worry about the difference.

Rai said he would look into it. Some days later when I asked again, I was told they couldn't get an organ for love or money anywhere in the country. As it happened, I had to go over to Canada that week. While there, I fixed up for an organ to be sent to Glasgow. Transport would eat up a good part of the saving, but I had to knock it into their heads. Later I could see progress. They were vying with one another to contrive productions with ingenuity rather than heavy cost.

Lewis Hynd still thinks I was mean in the prosperous years that followed. These were the years when having a television contract was likened—by me, I must admit—to having a 'licence to print money'. Perhaps this remark was injudicious but it was certainly right, and weren't certain people sorry now they'd refused to join me! As a matter of fact, I was not exaggerating. It was even better than I had ever imagined it would be. During the eight years we had an 80 per cent holding in Scottish Television until ITA forced us to reduce our holding first to 55 per cent and then to 25 per cent, our share of the company profits ran to £13m.

Lewis was wild because, every time he got a stack of money paid into the bank, he was told to transfer it to Fred Cusk, my financial director in London. Lewis felt that I might have spent more of the profits in Scotland, building new offices, perhaps, as other companies were doing in England, instead of always siphoning it off to the Thomson Newspapers. Actually, very little of the money that was being sent south originated in Scotland; the vast bulk of it came from detergent, cigarette, motor-car, sweets and consumer-durable firms buying network time in London.

What he may appreciate now is that, during the eight years, 1959 to 1967, every penny of that TV fortune, except for £393,750, went into the re-equipment of plant, the extension of premises and the building of much-needed new offices for various of our newspapers (including incidentally the antiquated Aberdeen office). Several millions of it went into finding a new office, equipping it to start a new evening paper, the first evening paper started since the war, with others to follow elsewhere. In fact, during that eight-year period which began about two years after STV started, we invested £31m. into plant and building to bring our provincial centres up to date, to give people in these centres greater security—and pride, too—in their jobs, to make our contribution to the improvement of the regions. And the £393,750? That was the sum total of all I ever sent out of this country. It was the sum I borrowed from Canada when I came here and bought the *Scotsman*. In eleven years that £393,750 had spilled over into Scottish Television and then into Kemsley Newspapers, and had, in fact, been very useful and profitable money.

I should add that although we spent that £31m. on plant improvement we will have one day soon to produce another £30m. for the rebuilding of the Blackburn and Belfast offices and the extension of other offices, besides a massive investment in the new printing techniques.

4

HOW TO MAKE A PRESS LORD

WHEN MY family were going to Florida every
winter (and I would join them for Christmas),
they or someone else persuaded me to buy a
yacht, the *Fairmile*, and one year, 1952, they or someone
else persuaded me to sail the *Fairmile* from Florida to
Nassau in the Bahamas. That was how I came to meet
Lord Beaverbrook. His yacht was there, so I went and
introduced myself to him and I had dinner with him two
nights running. He appeared to like me as a compatriot
who could talk about newspapers, and he came to lunch
with me and my family on the *Fairmile* and encouraged
me to buy a newspaper in Britain. It was on Max's
advice that I got myself invited later to Lord Kemsley's
country house, Dropmore, in Buckinghamshire, so that I
could sound him about buying his Aberdeen paper.
Kemsley said then that any of his papers could be bought
at the right price. Through Denis Hamilton, then his
chief assistant, he later conveyed to me the offer of the
Aberdeen paper at £2m. It was a calculated snub.

Never having attached much importance to snubs, I
approached Lord Kemsley again, seven years later over
luncheon, about his willingness to sell his Aberdeen
paper. By this time I was proprietor of the *Scotsman* and
chairman of Scottish Television, but I still had to listen to
Kemsley's ponderous and unfunny joke. The paper,

which earned only £100,000 a year, was offered to me this time for £2,500,000.

Yet seven weeks after that, Kemsley called me to the telephone one morning—1st July it was—and said he would like to see me. I was in the *Scotsman* office and I said warily, 'I'll come down next week.'

'That might be too late,' he said. I suggested that I could make the trip in two days' time, if it was so important. He then asked me point blank: 'Can't you come down tonight?'

I pondered this and asked him, 'Is it serious?'

'I think when I tell you what it is you'll consider it serious.'

Something in his quiet tone gave his words great gravity. 'I'll come down tonight,' I said, and we arranged a meeting in his office the next morning.

I hurried through to Jim Coltart's room and told him what had happened. I said I was sure that something big was afoot. It was so unlike Kemsley to come on the phone himself to persuade me. It called, I felt, for both of us to go down that night; I might well need Jim's support.

We discussed the possibility of Lord Kemsley wanting to sell more than the Aberdeen paper. Could he want to get rid of some of his other papers, too, and if so could we meet the price he would ask?

For the record, I must mention here that, having failed to interest Kemsley in a sale of the *Aberdeen Press & Journal*, I had approached George Outram & Co., proprietors of the *Glasgow Herald* and the *Evening Times*. Outram's had resisted all offers and we had then decided that, to get their papers, it was worth making a handsome takeover bid to the shareholders. In great secrecy a letter to every shareholder of Outram's had been prepared containing an offer for his shares. These letters were being put into envelopes at that very moment by

Ian Munro, the *Scotsman* company secretary. Jim Coltart told Ian to put the letters in the safe and await further instructions. Jim and I caught the night train for London.

We booked in at the Savoy and we had breakfast in a café in Covent Garden. I went with Jim to the Scottish Television office in Kingsway and from there took a taxi alone to Gray's Inn Road, where, at 10.45, Lord Kemsley was waiting.

This time, he was certainly serious. Without beating about the bush, he told me he wanted me to take over his whole newspaper group, Aberdeen, Middlesbrough, Blackburn, Newcastle, Sheffield, Manchester, Cardiff and London. Even his *Sunday Times*.

Kemsley had a 40 per cent holding in his company, a matter of one million shares. He said he wanted £6 a share, or £6m. There were a million and a half other shares. They were then about 42s. each on the market, but in accordance with the best city traditions he insisted that the other shareholders would have to be offered what he was offered.

I told him a deal like this was far beyond my capacity. I couldn't raise that kind of money.

Kemsley put his arm through mine and led me to the door, as if anxious to get rid of me before I could raise any more difficulties. 'Have you a financial adviser, a banker in London?'

I said that I dealt with S. G. Warburg's. 'Go to them,' he said. 'Tell them to get in touch with Lionel Fraser of Helbert Wagg's. They'll work something out together. Where are you staying?'

I told him.

'I'll be in touch,' he said, and dismissed me.

It was, of course, complete fantasy. Having made me the offer of one of the world's biggest newspaper chains, he dismissed me as if he were too busy and likewise too important to waste time with the likes of me.

I drove back to Kingsway telling myself that Kemsley was serious all right. He also seemed to be in a great hurry. His haste in getting rid of me was due to a great anxiety to get the negotiations started without delay.

What had happened in seven weeks to change the whole scene?

Kemsley Newspapers had already suffered one attempt to take them over. It had failed but it had scared Kemsley. Because of this, neither he nor any of his family dared sell any shares of the company. This was apparently causing problems for him, his four sons, his Mauritius-born wife and his step-daughter. Kemsley Newspapers Ltd. were earning about one-and-a-half million a year profit and as the family's shareholding was only 40 per cent and dividends had to be covered about twice, their take was not sufficient for their requirements. The style of living in both town and country house was expensive, and taxation was colossal. The death-duties situation in the event of his death would be critical.

Perhaps he had decided that he must settle things for his family before it was too late, must do the last big deal in a lifetime of financial dealing, so that he would have nothing more to worry about. Perhaps he was also afraid of a further shrinkage in the business. He had just come through a bad strike situation which seriously affected profitability. He had several bad losing papers which had to be closed or disposed of and this would present him with some serious headaches.

Having decided to sell, for whatever reason, he first of all decided to sell the group of Kemsley Newspapers, but to keep the *Sunday Times* going as his sole newspaper interest, which he believed was a possibility as, unlike his other papers, it was put together and printed at the *Daily Telegraph* office, owned by his nephews. Lionel Fraser looked into the proposition and told him bluntly that without the *Sunday Times* being included, he hadn't a hope of getting the money he wanted from the sale of his business. Gomer Berry, last of the three founders of the great Allied Newspapers empire, had to swallow his pride and throw his *Sunday Times* on to the market.

The problem was still sufficiently acute. Where were they to find one person or one group big enough and keen enough to take over the entire Kemsley outfit as an entity? One by one he had to pass over Cowdray, Beaverbrook, Cecil King and Rothermere who, he knew, would not be interested. So he came to me. And, having brought me in, what he had to do now was to find some way for me to raise the capital to buy him out. Since I had no hope of doing that, he or the financial men had to do it for me.

That much I was able to grasp and clarify in my mind on the taxi trip to the STV office in Kingsway, where Jim Coltart, all unsuspecting, was waiting. For obvious reasons, throughout the protracted negotiations that followed, the utmost caution was applied so that not a hint of what was going on could leak out. With my liking for telling everybody what I was doing, that was an ordeal for me, and the worst moment of the ordeal, I think,w as during those ten minutes when I met Jim and chatted to the office people and dared not say a word to Jim of what had happened. After that very long ten minutes, we got out to go to lunch. I recall we were on a Belisha crossing in Kingsway before I could take a chance and give him the sensational news. 'It's everything, Jim. He wants to sell everything—to me.'

'Not the *Sunday Times*!' Jim exclaimed.

'Everything.' This in the middle of the crowd crossing. Then on the further pavement, Jim still clinging to reality had to remember: 'What about Outram's?'

'That's off,' I said and we went to the nearest telephone kiosk and managed to put together enough coins to phone Edinburgh. Ian Munro came to the phone. 'Ian, those offers to Outram's shareholders. Not one has to go out of the office, do you understand? Lock them all up in the safe.'

'What's happened?'

'I'll tell you when we get back.'

'When will that be?'

'I don't know.' Jim rang off.

It was by a piece of extremely good timing that, some weeks previously, I had been introduced by Charles McQueen to Henry Grunfeld of S. G. Warburg, the merchant bank firm. It was Henry Grunfeld we now called on to conduct the negotiations on our behalf. It was Henry who was now to invent the 'reverse bid' take-over, by which Kemsley bought Scottish Television as the first step to being himself taken over. What clinched this first phase and indeed made the deal begin to look remotely possible was the valuation that these bankers, S. G. Warburg and Helbert Wagg, some of the shrewd-est men in the City, were able to put upon Scottish Television Ltd. My £400,000 company, for which only £160,000 had been invested and only £40,000 taken up in shares (£32,000 by me), had, in two years, become in their opinion worth £5,500,000. This £5½m. made it possible for the financial experts to start negotiations in earnest to transfer the properties of the Viscount Kemsley to the barber's son from Toronto.

The first nine days of these negotiations were the worst. Jim Coltart had to go back to Edinburgh after a week, in which, as he said afterwards, he was much impressed by, and indeed proud of, my ability to follow the ramifications of Henry Grunfeld's proposals and complicated suggestions. I moved into the Howard Hotel from the Savoy to get away from the chance of being recognized too often and also of running into someone who might also have seen me going into Helbert Wagg's office with Henry. It would have been too easy for a City journalist to put two and two together and it only needed a rumour to start a run on the Exchange.

The intervening weekend I spent in Edinburgh and took the opportunity on the Sunday morning to go round to Ian Macdonald's with the back of an old envelope covered with figures for Ian's edification, so that I could explain the situation so far as it had developed in the negotiations in Warburg's office.

The first problem confronting Lionel Fraser of Helbert Wagg's and Grunfeld was to persuade Lord Kemsley to reduce his price to £5 a share. This made the capitalisation needed of the order of £12½ million which in effect I would have to pay if all the shareholders as well as Lord Kemsley wanted cash. The first move was for Kemsley Newspapers to buy STV, paying me with £1m. in cash, £½m. in debentures, and a new issue of two million Kemsley shares. These shares, together with Lord Kemsley's million shares, would give me the control of the combined Kemsley Newspapers and Scottish Television. On that basis I could hope to raise the loan needed to pay Kemsley for his million shares.

What remained was the problem of the other Kemsley shareholders. If they all opted for £5 a share, where was that money to come from? Grunfeld then worked out a scheme by which the existing Kemsley shares in the hands of the public, other than those two million issued to pay me for STV, would be renamed 'preferred ordinary shares' and by being guaranteed an annual dividend of 30 per cent, would be made much more valuable than their present price on the Stock Exchange of 42s. Such an offer of a quick, high dividend in an STV-enriched Kemsley Newspapers company would, Grunfeld believed, lift the value of those old shares—the new preferred ordinaries—to about £5. Helbert Wagg then indicated that, this being the offer, they were prepared to underwrite it, Lord Kemsley agreeing to pay the costs involved.

Meanwhile my two million shares in Kemsley Newspapers, not being 'preferred ordinary' shares and not therefore having the guarantee of a 30 per cent dividend, would not rise above the 42s. price on the Exchange. This appeared also to put me out of voting control for there were two and a half million of the other shares to my two million. But for the £5m. which I was going to give Kemsley, I would receive his million shares. Thus I would receive another million votes and the other shareholders' total would be reduced to one and a half million.

I would then have complete control of the new Kemsley Newspapers-Scottish Television set-up. All I needed, as I explained to Ian Macdonald, was the £5m. to pay Lord Kemsley.

In fact, what I needed was £4m., since there had been a million of cash included in the £5½m. given me in the first instance as the purchase price of STV by Kemsley Newspapers. For that deal I was to get the two million shares, specially issued and valued at £4m., and £1m. in cash and £½m. in debentures. That £1m. in cash would now go to Lord Kemsley personally and stay with him. Then I believed that I could satisfy him as to a second £1m. by giving him promissory notes from Thomson Scottish Associates, which was a company we would form to control STV and the *Scotsman*. That left £3m. to be found. It was a lot to ask, but for a big deal a lot was needed. Would Ian and his bank find this cash for me?

This was really the crux of the whole deal. There was no other way of getting the controlling shares without buying them from Kemsley and no other way of paying Kemsley without raising a £3m. loan, and there was no other bank I could approach for such a sum.

I never imagined such a moment would come in my

life, that I would be strolling in an Edinburgh Braid Hills garden on a warm July Sunday at the age of 65, the official age of retirement, asking a banker for the loan of £3m. What was probably even more surprising was that I got it.

Ian, of course, would have to refer such a loan to a directors' meeting. But he gave me the assurance that morning that I would get the money if the Kemsley deal went through. I could take his word for it and go ahead.

I suppose it was at that moment that I first realized it could happen; that I could get possession of the whole Kemsley chain of British newspapers. Contracts and agreements had still to be drawn up to embrace legally all Henry Grunfeld's sophisticated scheming, the offer for the shares had still to be made successfully, but now it looked as if nothing in the due processes of the Stock Exchange and the financial laws of the country would stop me becoming the owner of three national Sunday papers, thirteen provincial dailies and several weeklies and a provincial Sunday—in fact one of the Big Four newspaper owners of Britain—unless it was a premature leak of the news.

The biggest newspaper news of the century was being made under the noses of Fleet Street and not a glimmer of it must get out or the whole deal would be ruined. If there was a run on the Stock Exchange for Kemsley shares we were finished. As the negotiations were resumed on the Monday morning, I began to develop the anxieties of a broody hen. These negotiations had already involved so many people, so many consultations with experts, that I grew terrified that someone along the line would drop an unfortunate word, someone would get wind of the deal and dive into the Stock Market to make a fortune. Worse than that, if anything could be worse, I feared the relentless high-pressure activities of the *Express* reporters and City men. How gleefully Beaverbrook would pounce on the news of his old rival having to sell! And that very Tuesday, in the *Daily Express*, apparently for no reason at all, was an article about me!

Every time I came out of the small hotel I was now staying in, or out of Warburg's office, I was sure I was being followed. Would they see me meeting Fraser and spot the Kemsley connection?

I couldn't stand the suspense. I now calculated the risk of the Beaver getting on to this news. It was too real. I called him on the telephone. I told him what was going on and I put it to him straight: 'Max, for God's sake, don't muck it up.'

He gave me his promise immediately. 'Roy, I'm with you all the way.'

I trusted him and he did not fail me.

But a few days later another spectre hovered high above the new buildings and the bomb sites of the City as I taxied between meetings. Now that the deal had been thrashed out and all the snags circumvented, the Kemsley group were obliged to announce that negotiations with Roy Thomson had begun.

Might not someone intervene in the takeover situation, make a bigger offer? There were immediate rumours that Charles Clore and Lord Cowdray were both interested, were consulting their bankers. Nothing could stop either of them topping the bid for the Kemsley shares if they wished. Could it possibly have been in Kemsley's mind, as he reduced his price, that this might happen, that he might be offered more?

Of course this was not so. But I was equally sure that snags could arise by the dozen. It was going to take a month for the agreement to be printed and signed, the offers to go out and return, the cheques to be signed and handed over.

It may have been that the worst danger, and that completely unpredictable, arose through my own carelessness.

I had to go off to Canada, and as I was leaving I was implored by Jim Coltart to keep a tight clamp on anything controversial when the reporters came out in force at the airport. 'No comment' was not exactly my style. Some of these boys were Thomson men. They wouldn't let me go and I dare say I agreed with one suggestion flung at me that, as a Canadian, I surely had found the newspapers in Britain bogged down by old-fashioned ways, and I surely was looking forward to tackling the difficulties which, in recent years, had been mounting in the Kemsley offices. I believe that all I ever said on these points was 'Yes, I suppose so,' but the two statements were printed as coming from me—'Old-fashioned ways' and 'Kemsley difficulties'. Put them together and you see that they were well calculated to offend a proud man like Lord Kemsley.

I got an angry cable from Kemsley himself, demanding an explanation. There was a phone call from Jim saying it was serious. 'Lord Kemsley is such a proud old so-and-so he's quite capable of pulling out of the deal.' I realized that this was indeed a possibility, however astonishing. Gomer Berry, once his Welsh blood was roused by what he took to be an insult, was capable of throwing my beautiful dreams out of the window.

I went to work at once, calling my friends in various Canadian newspaper offices. I persuaded the paper which particularly featured the damaging statements to print an admission that I had been misquoted. This, thank God, was the difference between London and Toronto. In London, if anything had been published that impugned the journalist's accuracy, there would have been a strike or a court case. In Canada the newsdesk laughed when they heard what had happened and assured me that 'Al won't give a darn if we publish a denial, not if it really saves you. No one will believe it here, anyway.'

I cabled the full text of the denial as printed to Lord

Kemsley and added my apologies for getting into a position in which I could be misreported. The crisis lasted only twenty-four hours but they were twenty-four nasty hours for me. At last Jim called me that Kemsley seemed mollified. I swore I would talk to no more newsmen.

We paid a final call upon Lord Kemsley in his office on Friday afternoon, 21st August, 1959. This was a formal occasion, since the final details had all been settled. Now that the time had come to go, Gomer genuinely wanted our assurance that everything would be done right for the staffs and the papers in the empire from which he was reluctantly abdicating.

I told him then, quite sincerely, that I would feel humble when I occupied his chair.

'You needn't worry about that,' Kemsley replied, with the glint of a half-smile. 'You won't be occupying it. It's not a company chair and I'm taking it with me.' He did, too.

That was Gomer Berry, a great newspaper financier, who had so successfully managed and found the capital for the numerous and bold newspaper promotions of his brothers and himself, having started from quite modest beginnings. Later that day he was alone in his room on the third floor of Gray's Inn Road for the last hour. In adjoining rooms and in the corridor outside directors and assistants instinctively moved quietly, hoping to spare the old man any incident that would add to his emotional strain. Much to everyone's surprise he was heard laughing outright in his room. Someone, it transpired, had told him that Roy Thomson and James Coltart would be arriving at the office on the Monday at nine o'clock. Nine o'clock! What an absurd hour to take over the reins from him! And he would be far away . . .

Having given instructions for the removal of his desk, which he also regarded as a personal possession and at which he had no intention of letting Roy Thomson sit, Lord Kemsley departed. His parting gift to Denis Hamilton, his chief assistant and editorial director, who had been with him for thirteen years, was a photocopy of a cheque for £3½m. payable to Viscount Kemsley by S. G. Warburg, this being the £5m. due from me, less the £1m. he had agreed to receive over ten years and the £500,000 costs of underwriting the offer (to other shareholders) which he had undertaken.

Jim Coltart and I took a Sunday train from Edinburgh on 23rd August and at eight the next morning were breakfasting in the friendly café patronized by fruit porters. We were at the Coley Street door of what was still Kemsley House by five minutes to nine. This was the door which only certain executives had been allowed to use and where, when a phone call was received in the mornings, informing the commissionaire that the car had just departed, a chain was immediately put upon the lift gate so that no one could use it; nothing must prevent it being wide open and welcoming for the viscount. One of the two commissionaires who met us that morning had to ring the bell for the lift, the other whipped my case from my hand before I could resist. There was barely room for all four of us in that lift, the two commissionaires being corpulent men, heavily uniformed and bemedalled. When we got to the third floor we were met by a third immaculate doorman. We had never been used to this sort of thing, for which the *Scotsman* accountants, even in the old days, would not have stood. 'Have we taken over the British Legion?' Jim asked as we were at last left alone in Kemsley's big corner room and the door shut behind us. Thus began the biggest takeover in British newspaper history.

A certain sense of being there under false pretences affected both of us. We walked into the adjoining board-room and examined the pictures, and I said, 'I tell you what: let's see what all the directors are paid.' We were joined then by Ivor Charles, who had been waiting for our call. He had been Kemsley's personal assistant and was going to be mine. He said that Wheadon, the company secretary, would be in presently, which he was. Ivor Wheadon fetched us the salary lists. He also informed us that some of the family directors would not be in the office, it being mid-August, and Lord Kemsley having insisted that they all rejoin their families by the seaside, all the excitement being by his reckoning over, but all the non-family directors were available.

That salary list was an eye-opener to us, though it is fair to say that it was the first time we had seen a London newspaper's top-rank payroll. 'They'll have to be good,' Jim said. Then I said I'd like to know how many company cars were being used by these people. This was a second list we were bound to shake our heads over, for not only did the members of the Berry family who were directors each have a Rolls or a Bentley (and a chauffeur) but also very often their families had the use of other company vehicles; one granddaughter, who worked on one of the papers, had a Jaguar for her personal use. So we wrote out an instruction for Ivor Wheadon to send out that day: as from the 1st of September no one in the company would retain more than one car. As an afterthought we added that all Rolls-Royces would be returned to the company garage and would be replaced by Rovers. This caused more distress among the members of Lord Kemsley's family than anything else we did then or later. They all wrote asking us to give them a little time and they would buy the cars from us.

Kemsley's four sons were staying on as directors of the firm, Lionel as deputy chairman, Denis in charge of the Newcastle office, Neville in an indiscriminate capacity and Anthony at Cardiff. Lord Kemsley had asked me to agree to keep them on for a couple of years. The four executive directors, Angus Burnett-Stuart, Eric Cheadle, Denis Hamilton and Michael Renshaw, all came to me and asked for contracts. This wasn't surprising, considering how suddenly Kemsley had left them without any protection whatsoever, and in fact none of them in later years ever asked for these contracts to be renewed.

What we had to make clear from the start was that not only was Jim to be Managing Director but that he was to manage the business. I asked him then how he proposed to operate. He said we should have two boards, the parent board under my chairmanship deciding the strategy of the company and approving the main decisions of the executive board, of which he would be chairman, with the four executive directors as members.

'What about Lionel?' I asked.

'We can't have him on the executive board. We can't have you as chairman, and we can't have your deputy.'

'You'll have trouble if you try to run the company without him.'

'Will you leave me to handle Lionel?' Jim asked.

He told me later that Lionel had protested when he was not asked to attend a meeting of the executive board. He had always taken executive decisions in the company when his father was too busy or was absent.

'You'd be embarrassed now,' Jim told him.

'Embarrassed? Why?'

'Because we are, for instance, going to discuss the position of your cousin at Sheffield.'

'What about him?'

'Well, Sheffield is losing money at the rate of £100,000 a year. I understand Mr. Berry arrives at the office every morning accompanied by his two Borzois. His only previous experience of taking command, I believe, was during his career in the Guards. Well, now he is going to be replaced and I shall offer him a job here in London where he can, if he likes, learn something about management.'

'I see what you mean,' Lionel said, and agreed that he would be satisfied if Jim had lunch with him once a week and filled him in with details of what was being done.

The next thing we discovered was that the brothers continued to correspond with one another about company affairs and take decisions as they had always done about various things. Denis, in Newcastle, had always been in overall charge of machinery and plant, and he was still being contacted from Aberdeen and Cardiff and even London with requests for new purchases and replacements. Out had to go another directive letter, this time laying it down that no purchase over a certain amount would be made without the decision of the executive board.

Lionel was very nice about it. 'This isn't going to work,' he predicted, and two months later the sons all sent in their resignations and departed.

It was really surprising to us that there were so few departures from among the old Kemsley executives after we took over, and I must say that although I thought the company, regarded as a commercial undertaking, had been too benevolently run, I had begun to like Lord Kemsley and I was sorry that, after leaving Gray's Inn Road, he cut himself off from us. I was to see just how much time and skill he had devoted to the *Sunday Times* and it was in every way in sound condition at the time of our takeover. The staff of the *Sunday Times* in the editorial, advertising and other departments were excellent and I had to make few changes over the years.

One of these was when Harry Hodson left the editor's chair to become Provost of Ditchley a year after I arrived. I persuaded a rather reluctant Denis Hamilton to be editor and he took that on as well as continuing to be editorial director of the regional papers for two years. In a very few years the sale of the paper was increased to 1,500,000.

In Kemsley's Aberdeen office we discovered an executive with whom we had parted company in Edinburgh. When we took over the *Scotsman*, we did not reckon the general manager, John Noble, as being suitable for our style of operating. Noble had done a stout job trying to manage the *Scotsman* and the *Scotsman* owners together. To be able to control the owner and his partners, a paid employee required a certain amount of character and strength of will, which were not likely to endear him to Jim Coltart or me. Accordingly John Noble departed, and here, now, we discovered him in charge of our Aberdeen office.

In Aberdeen the figures did not look good. The profit had gone from £160,000 to £80,000 and then to £28,000 in the last three years. It wasn't a question of capabilities, but we felt we needed new blood. So this time we had to deal with John's lawyers. We weren't willingly going to pay him compensation every time we parted company.

But once these details of every-day working arrangements were settled, we found that the country-wide organization that we had taken over worked reasonably well. No one of our determined natures needed to be afraid of running fifteen newspapers if we could successfully run three (as a matter of fact we had not yet got Edinburgh into profit). Jim Coltart says that the reason the directors I had taken over from Kemsley stayed with us and worked so loyally for the new company was not that I was exactly lavish in the rewards I put their way, but that I quite delighted them with the trust I put in them; once having seen how they worked and the capabilities they had, I told them to do things their own way, not to trouble giving me details, we all had plenty to do. Kemsley had hated delegating anything and these men now felt as if they had come of age. I have always known that other men could run a business as well as I could, perhaps better, so long as the figures and the forecasts came to me. I have never gone about worrying over what someone might be doing to my business, unless I found something that looked wrong, and that always comes out in the figures. Now I was pleased to let Kemsley's executive directors get on with it, while I began to figure what would improve the company and what we should do next. I had time to do some figuring on the backs of envelopes.

5

ABUSE OF AN INNOCENT TYCOON

BEFORE THE end of the year, our complacency was shattered. We had three months in which to consider the changes we should introduce into the chain of Kemsley newspapers to put the business on a better footing. Then the blow fell.

On Thursday, 17th December, 1959, that year of great moment in the history of newspapers, the secretary of the *Daily Telegraph* wrote to the secretary of Thomson Newspapers Ltd. giving six months' notice of termination of the contract to print the *Sunday Times*. The last issue of the *Sunday Times* to be printed in the Fleet Street office of the *Daily Telegraph*, he wrote, would be the issue of 12th June, 1960.

No one in the newspaper business would have believed that the printing presses capable of running off more than seven hundred thousand copies of a forty-page *Sunday Times* (the rest being printed in Manchester) could be installed in Thomson House, and run in as they ought to be, within six months. Or within a year, for that matter. Or that such presses could be found in some other office ready, capable and willing to take over.

That letter from the *Daily Telegraph* was a body blow. On the face of it, and being as optimistic as may be, it meant that the *Sunday Times* was being put out of circulation for a few months. Whether the paper would survive such an enforced hiatus, what sort of circulation it would pick up when it was restarted, after its readers had in the meantime formed the habit of buying some other paper, were questions that no one could very plausibly answer.

That letter followed very swiftly a meeting I had had with Michael Berry. Two things had been worrying me particularly about the Sunday situation that we had taken over. One was that the *Sunday Graphic* was a loss-maker and wasn't likely to be anything else. The other was that the *Sunday Times* could easily be making more money, for it was by no means taking all the advertising that it could be. So I met Michael Berry on 14th December and told him what I had in mind. I asked how soon could he adapt and enlarge his printing presses in Fleet Street so that we could have a forty-eight-page *Sunday Times*? It would take years, he said, and he doubted if it would ever be feasible, since presses so big would not be needed by the *Daily Telegraph*.

I thought I was discussing this on a friendly basis. After all, he was Kemsley's nephew and his company had printed the *Sunday Times* since 1937, since, in fact, they had ceased to have a share in it. Our enterprises had always been linked, first by blood ties and then by mutual interest. So I suggested to him that, if it wouldn't be feasible to enlarge the presses at Fleet Street, his company might consider coming to Gray's Inn Road, where, apart from the press-room which I would have to refit, there would be office space, since I was going to complete the building which his uncle had begun and which was still only in the half-finished state in which it had been halted by the war. Very likely I would have to stop the *Sunday Graphic* and print the *Sunday Times* there instead, which meant that there would be spare capacity during the week which would be economical for him to use, and no doubt he could make a lot of money leasing or selling his Fleet Street plant. He said he and his brother would consider this proposition, though he felt they did not really want to change.

I then asked him if they would consider selling their business to me. This was what I said to everybody, but, of course, the *Daily Telegraph* would have suited me very well. I was surprised when he appeared to flush with annoyance and cut the interview short. So no doubt I was partly to blame for what followed. As I have said the suggestion of buying a family-owned newspaper is often received as an insult and no doubt mortally offended the Berrys. I was quite brash in my approach and there was some excuse for him resenting what I did.

Four days later the notice terminating the contract for printing the *Sunday Times* in the *Daily Telegraph* office dropped on Ivor Wheadon's desk. Michael Berry also wrote to me personally:

'My brother and I have discussed your proposal that the *Daily Telegraph* should share premises with your organisation at Gray's Inn Road. After full consideration we have decided that we do not wish to avail ourselves of your offer. As regards the enlargement of printing facilities here, I regret to inform you that it will be several years before we shall be able to print larger sizes of the *Sunday Times*. We realise this will be unacceptable to you and you will want to remove the *Sunday Times* to your own premises. In view of approaches we have had, we cannot accept an indeterminate date for this move and are accordingly giving you six months' notice of termination of the contract now.'

One thing I hadn't realized when dealing with Michael Berry was that he had every reason to dislike what his uncle, Kemsley, had done. Unknown to me, it had been agreed between Lord Kemsley and his brother, Lord

Camrose, when they divided the Allied Newspapers company into two separate concerns, that if either of them wanted to sell, he should give the other first offer. This Kemsley had not done, nor had he even warned Michael Berry of what he was doing. Perhaps he felt that, his brother being dead, the promise he had made to him no longer held good. Perhaps he had felt that he dared not give any inkling of his intention. He had indeed sprung a complete surprise on his nephews, who would not have believed that he would sell the *Sunday Times*.

No doubt the Berrys had immediately begun to think of what I would do with the *Sunday Times*; no doubt they had made a shrewd guess. Sooner or later, I was going to renounce the contract and print the *Sunday Times* at Gray's Inn Road. What then were they going to do with their presses on a Saturday night except produce a *Sunday Telegraph* as they had often talked about doing? And if it had to come to that, was it not better that it came at a time that would put me at a disadvantage rather than them?

We sent for the files of Kemsley printing contracts and correspondence and began meticulously to go through them, though without any hope of finding a loop-hole. There was a note from the *Daily Telegraph* in October 1943, drawing attention to the expiry of the 1937 agreement on the 13th of that month, which agreement stated that 'it will continue thereafter until terminated by one party giving the other six calender months' notice in writing. Unless I hear from you I will presume that the contract will be continued.'

That seemed to settle the matter. Then, attached to that letter, we found a short note:

'Lord Kemsley telephoned in acknowledging my reminder, and said that he is going to let the agreement carry on, but so far as he recollects he arranged for the notice to be twelve months instead of six.'

There was then a note from Lord Kemsley confirming this and the existence of a supplemental agreement of 1937 in which the twelve months' notice was stipulated. It was a discovery that lifted us at once out of our despondency. Before he gave us the six months' notice, Michael Berry must have had the agreement checked. Whoever did the checking had come across that wartime letter mentioning the six months' notice 'in writing' that would be required to terminate the agreement and had not bothered to search further. He obviously had not come across the addendum making the notice twelve months.

Denis Hamilton told me at the time that there had been a tremendous row between Lord Kemsley and Michael Berry some years before about the price of the Amalgamated Press shares when Seymour and Michael Berry sold their periodical interests to Odhams. Lord Kemsley as trustee for the Buckland family felt aggrieved that these family shares were not being bought at the same price as Michael was receiving. 'There will be trouble when I am dead,' Kemsley said to Denis. 'They may start up in opposition. I am going to get extended notice in the printing contract.'

Twelve months' notice would now give us a fair chance. We might manage to get the presses installed in a year, though there wasn't a hope of having them properly tested and tried out—'proved' as they say in the trade. Every extra day we could win would be a godsend. Ivor Wheadon was instructed to wait until the 21st of December before writing to the *Telegraph* and then merely to acknowledge the two letters and to say that I was in Canada.

He then waited two weeks and wrote on 4th January: 'The notice of termination of the contract cannot be accepted as it is not in accordance with the terms of our agreement with you.'

80

Nothing came back by return. We waited till the next day. Still nothing. We were counting every day. In the meantime the experts had come in, planning had started to convert some of the old presses, extending them to take the full size of the *Sunday Times,* and contracts and plans were being worked on for the new presses we would need in such a hurry. Every day we gained without that letter might be the one extra day we would so desperately need twelve months hence. We could not understand why the *Daily Telegraph* did not reply. The twelve months' notice which they must now give us could only begin from the day it was given.

On legal advice, Wheadon wrote again on 13th January; this time he asked for acknowledgement of his letter of 4th January.

What kind of confusion had set in at the *Telegraph* office? We will never know. For on the 22nd—nine days later—I wrote to Michael Berry, acknowledging his letter of 17th December, and asking for his views on our letter of 4th January. Finally, but even now not until the 25th, the secretary of the *Daily Telegraph* wrote to the secretary of Thomson Newspapers Ltd. regretting the overlooking of the agreement which amended the original contract and now giving twelve months' notice. The last edition of the *Sunday Times* to be printed in the *Daily Telegraph* office would now be not the issue of 12th June, 1960, as they had first said but that of Sunday, 22nd January, 1961.

Not only an extra six months had been gained, but because of our slight delay in drawing their attention to the error, and the *Daily Telegraph's* failure to alter the notice quickly, another four weeks had been given us to plan the new presses, get them made and installed.

In the event we just scrambled home. On 22nd January we printed our last copy in Fleet Street. That Sunday, soon after we had gone to press, the equipment, type and other gear in the composing room at Fleet Street were moved across to Gray's Inn Road by the compositors themselves. Working on the Sunday, they planned the move like a military operation. Meanwhile the rushed installation of the big presses at Gray's Inn Road was barely completed. And it was a 'damned close-run thing' if ever there was. Those four extra weeks that we gained were, as it turned out, absolutely crucial. We couldn't have produced a *Sunday Times* at Gray's Inn Road a week earlier than we did. As it was, the usual proofing period for such machinery, which was several months, had to be dispensed with. The result was a time of considerable teething troubles. But the paper never missed publication, never gave any widespread encouragement to readers to lose the habit of reading it, which of course is the grave danger of strikes or stoppages in the newspaper industry.

Though I had this trouble over these events that led to the *Sunday Telegraph*'s arrival, I see much to admire in Michael Berry (now Lord Hartwell). I think his handling of the *Daily Telegraph* has always been of the highest editorial quality, and he was certainly a brave man to start a newpaper in a field which in the end will probably not support three quality Sundays. He has been resolute at great cost recently in standing up to hotheads who have hit the *Daily Telegraph* production.

I have been friendly with all the proprietors and leading figures of Fleet Street since 1959. They are as varied a set of men as you could possibly create, from second- and third-generation figures such as the highly experienced Lord Rothermere and his son, Vere, the second generation Sir Max Aitken, the extremely able and charming Lord Drogheda and the newcomer, Rupert Murdoch, who is now concentrating on opening up in the United States.

In the meantime, being a newcomer in London was a

very different experience from being the new *Scotsman* proprietor in Edinburgh. My diary for the last months of 1959 has dates in it to attend a reception at No. 10 and meet the Prime Minister, to dine with Lord Beaverbrook and then with Lord and Lady Rosebery, to appear on *Panorama*, to lunch with Cecil King, to lunch with the German ambassador and meet Chancellor Adenauer, to go to a reception at the Gaitskells, to visit the famed Marquess of Salisbury. The top people in British life were curious to meet the new proprietor of the *Sunday Times*.

For the time being, I lived in London in a small hotel. I wasn't in a hurry to get myself a house in England. As a matter of fact I had bought a villa in the South of France first. This was found for me by Lord Beaverbrook, tootling about the narrow winding roads of Cap d'Ail in his converted London taxi. He was quite determined that I should be a neighbour of his out there and he was a difficult man to resist.

I said to myself: 'I can afford it. I can afford to fly out even for weekends, as I used to do in Florida, and get a bit of sun and sea air. I don't need to work so hard in London.' Actually it was months before I went out there even to see the place. Gunther and Hanni had moved to Cap d'Ail from Edinburgh and a number of people went as my guests. But me—well, even at weekends there was always something I wanted to figure out on my own.

From the start I was frequently on television. For a television interview with Randolph Churchill (and later for *Face to Face* with John Freeman) I took a good deal of pains. Right at that time my appearance and my performance on television were going to impress a small number of people who mattered and a lot of people who might buy Thomson Newspaper shares. Everyone, including TV critics next morning, said how relaxed and calm I had been with Randolph, in spite of his attempts at provocation, at which he was not untalented. In fact I had spent a number of hours that day and the previous day being grilled by some of my sharpest colleagues in Gray's Inn Road. I got them to fire questions at me, the kind of questions they thought I would be asked, and I got them to note the answers I gave that they didn't think good or even adequate, then we went over these again and again. I had had enough experience of radio in Canada to know that a good performance doesn't come by chance, or as the actor said, 'To play a big scene well, you've got to have chalk marks on the stage.' In any case I had to know what really concerned the English public at that time and to memorize my best lines on the really burning topics. It was a certain satisfaction to learn a little later that my rating went fairly high with the TV men.

Randolph was, in fact, a formidable interlocutor and he cornered me into saying one thing I regretted: that if the only way to stop the *Empire News* going out of business was by publishing spicier news and spicier articles, I might go along with that.

'Even although you are a very rich man?'

'I wouldn't be doing it for the profit. I'd be doing it for my employees.'

There was nothing wrong with that but I felt uncomfortable about it. I felt altogether unhappy about the *Empire News*. In a subsequent television interview I told Keith Waterhouse, when he quoted my answer to Randolph, 'If I said that, then I've changed my mind, because I don't intend to do it.'

A month or two later we completed negotiations with Sir William Carr of the *News of the World*, whose contract for having his northern editions printed by the *News Chronicle* was coming to an end. To take over that contract at Withy Grove, Manchester, we had to stop the *Empire News* and Sir William bought that paper to merge it with his, taking over its million and a half readers, taking care also of a great many employees. This was a very beneficial arrangement for us. For, in fact, the *Empire News* had not been paying; it was a strange time, indeed, in which a newspaper with a circulation of almost a million and a half could not pay its way. That was what labour and paper costs and television advertising had done to another Kemsley paper.

And I was glad to be appearing on further radio and television programmes at this time, for it was important to let the public know that I wasn't merging and closing down papers without very good reason. Vanity doesn't really come into this. A million and a half shares owned by the public kept their value because the public liked the look of my face and the straightforwardness of my approach to business.

Even today, when I'd much rather stay at home, I am always ready to make a journey, sometimes abroad, to attend the centenary celebration of a newspaper, or the opening of a hotel, or a travel agents' convention in Majorca, to go on television, and to be very careful of that, to rehearse thoroughly what I am going to say, so that I can put over to the public what we stand for and what we are going to do. In this, I am doing the best I can for the shareholders of my organisation, and saying that isn't being hypocritical. Of course if the shares keep buoyant as the result of my speech or appearance, my family trusts benefit. But the price of those shares matters perhaps even more to the widow with two thousand of them.

Talking about widows . . . One of the people I met at Donaghadee, while spending a weekend there in Northern Ireland with Cyril Lord of carpet fame, was a Mrs. Lee, the widow of the proprietor of the *Belfast Telegraph*, whose young son had inherited 66 per cent of the company shares, these being held in a trust as he was a minor. They had a problem, for £312,375 had been borrowed from the paper to pay the death duties. I told her I was interested in buying the paper but I learned that there was a snag.

She arranged for me to meet her solicitor, Mr. D. W. McMaster, and the two trustees, and from them I got the first hint of the trouble to come. The *Telegraph* company had articles of association which, to my Canadian eyes, looked very peculiar.

They laid down that if any shareholder wished to sell shares notice must be given to the Board who would then have a full month to find a purchaser (who might seem acceptable—or amenable—to them) and the price to be paid should be fixed by three outside arbitrators appointed by the Board. The seller would have no say in the price the shares were to be sold at nor to whom they would be sold. Only if the Board failed to find such a purchaser of their choice within one month would the seller be free to bargain for what he, or she, might reckon a good or even a fair price.

When this clause was first drafted into the articles of association—in 1896—it no doubt seemed much less strange to the owner of that time. He may indeed have devised it in order to prevent any vestige of the political and religious antagonisms which bedevilled Ulster life from penetrating into the company. The *Telegraph* had remained from that time staunchly Unionist and Protestant. Even the compositors objected when a later editor prepared to publish an interview with Jack Lynch, Prime Minister of the Irish Republic.

I had had no idea, of course, what formidable characters were opposed to me when I put my innocent toe tentatively into these dark waters. The *Telegraph* board set-up was also, to say the least, somewhat peculiar. R. M. Sayers had taken over the position of Chairman, which Robert Baird had held until his death. Sayers was also

Managing Director and his nephew, John E. Sayers, like his father and his uncle before him, was editor, though in his case joint editor with another man, an odd arrangement I had never come across before. Neither R.M. nor J. E. Sayers owned any shares in the company. They were not, however, without power.

The biggest shareholding, held in trust for the son, who could not inherit until he was thirty, had been represented on the Board by Mr. Bailey of Hill, Vellacott and Bailey, the auditors, but Mr. Bailey had been denied re-election by a ruling of Mr. Sayers that even when coming up for re-election directors must first be approved by the Board.

This approval had been refused after a vote. Later, however, the two trustees, Samuel George and William Bradley, had gone to law on this matter, and R. M. Sayers had yielded. The two trustees were elected to the Board.

George and Bradley were middle executives of the company, one being Circulation Manager and the other Cashier, and they had little say in the running of the affairs of the paper. They had been nominated as trustees by the late Robert Baird.

In any case, there was considerable ill-feeling between them and the other directors, and between Mrs. Lee and the rest of the Board (of which she, too, was a member). This was the peculiar situation: that none of the members of the Board had any financial interest in the company, and the trustees and Mrs. Lee, who were at least associated with the main shareholder, claimed during the subsequent proceedings, that they did not have confidence in the Chairman.

That late autumn in 1960, I realized that the clause relating to the sale of shares must be eliminated from the articles of association, otherwise no one would be allowed to seek or to get the best price for their shares. To remove that clause would require by law 75 per cent of the votes. Apart from the trust for the son, which as I have said held 66 per cent of the shares, the two sisters of the late owner held 17 per cent each. One of these sisters would have to vote with the trustees to get the articles of association altered.

On Mr. McMaster's advice I approached Mrs. Wilkinson, one of the sisters, who we believed would be very happy to be able to realize some of her capital, and I explained to her how she would have to back the trustees if she wanted to have freedom to sell her shares at the best price obtainable. She had heard of an offer having been made to the Board of £15 a share (by Alec Jeans of the *Liverpool Post*) but she had been given a valuation of £18 by auditors. I told her then that, if the articles were altered, and she was free and willing to sell to me, I would pay her £20. This seemed to her, and indeed was, a generous price.

I then met the trustees, Mrs. Lee and the solicitor, Mr. McMaster. It should be noted that I never did anything throughout this whole business without at all times making sure that the people concerned had their lawyer present. On this occasion, in the Grand Central Hotel, Belfast, I told them of my verbal agreement with Mrs. Wilkinson and that she would give them the necessary majority to get the articles altered. I said I would give them, too, £20 a share and they agreed this was a generous price.

Mr. McMaster then sent for his secretary and began to draft an agreement between us. At the request of the trustees I added a guarantee to maintain R. M. Sayers' pension entitlement and also that I would pay Mrs. Lee a sum of £25,000 to replace the £2,000 which each year the Board had voted her. This, as a capital payment, they hoped would be tax-free.

We waited for the agreements to be typed, so that we

could sign them there and then, since it might be difficult for me to get back to Belfast at an early date. While waiting, I assured the two trustees that I would maintain continuity of employment at the *Telegraph* and, in earnest of this, I offered both Sam George and William Bradley a new contract. They had been earning £2,000 and £1,850 respectively (not, of course, counting their directors' fees) and I said they should each have a £400 increase and the contract would be for fifteen years. In retrospect, although I meant this to be an assurance, I don't think it was fair to bind them for fifteen years at what was really a fairly low salary.

We got Mr. McMaster to draw up service contracts and these as well as the agreements on the shares were all signed that day, 4th November. The date is important.

Next day, back in London, I received a phone call from Mr. McMaster saying that he had taken opinion about the payment to Mrs. Lee and to make it taxable as a capital profit rather than as income, the agreement would have to be redrafted. I readily agreed that I would sign a new agreement if he sent it to me and tear up the old one. This I did and the new agreement about Mrs. Lee and also about the sale of the shares was dated 7th November.

As I have said, the *Belfast Telegraph* was, of long standing, a stout pillar of the Unionist establishment of Ulster. The first reaction to any proposed transfer of its ownership was political rather than commercial. In these first weeks after the signing of that agreement, no one was worrying about the minor whose shares were going to be sold. But it can be imagined that there was alarm in the bridge-playing echelons of the establishment when it was known that a bid was possible from someone like me, unpledged in Ulster politics and already becoming notorious for giving my editors complete freedom of editorial opinion.

The rumour of my active interest in the *Telegraph* was soon circulating. It could well have reached Alec Jeans in Liverpool or, more likely, he was spoken to by R. M. Sayers, who would have considered him a more desirable purchaser than myself. Sayers and the Ulster establishment certainly did not want an open-minded Scots Canadian taking over. Open minds were not appreciated in Ulster then. Sayers may also have been worried about his job and his nephew's future. Jeans, it was believed in Belfast, said that he could not top my offer of £20, but it was pointed out to him that he could make a tentative offer by mail of £21 and as he would not put up a cash deposit (as I had done) he could withdraw this offer at any time.

That was on 11th November. There was another offer, which came unexpectedly from another newspaper, the figure being £22 10*s*, but this bid did not seem to be taken seriously. In fact, in their affidavits to the court, Sam George and William Bradley said:

'We verily believe that these offers [Jeans's and the other paper's] were not made with any genuine intention that they should be accepted, but merely with a view to embarrassing us and in the hope that they might lead to proceedings such as the present.'

The trustees may also have had in mind that I had paid in £400,000 as a deposit on my bid, whereas other bidders had put no money at risk to support their offers. In addition I had agreed to buy Mrs. Wilkinson's shares for £291,800, so that I had at risk £691,800. I met Alec Jeans in London at this time and he pointed out how much I had at risk, whereas he had none, he said, and besides I would have to face a lawsuit. I might well end up, he thought, with only a minority holding (Mrs. Wilkinson's shares) for my £691,800.

On the 7th December the articles of association were

duly altered at an extraordinary general meeting of the company. As my policy in taking over a newspaper was wherever possible to own 100 per cent, I then wrote to Mrs. Bellairs, the other sister of the previous owner, offering her the same price for her shares. She put me in touch with her solicitor, a Mr. Rankin, who met me at the Grand Central. I had with me the documents, copies of my agreements with the trustees and Mrs. Lee and of my contracts with the two men, George and Bradley. Not having anything to hide, I let him see these, to show how much I was paying the other shareholders and to demonstrate my intention to give the *Telegraph* continuity of employment.

We were now getting into deeper waters. For there was a discrepancy of dates between the documents. It appeared that I had given George and Bradley their new contracts on 4th November and come to an agreement about the selling of the shares and the price on 7th November (because *that* agreement had had to be re-drafted). This discrepancy could have been explained to Mr. Rankin in a few words, if he had asked me. Mr. Rankin did not happen to ask me. From this point stemmed all the trouble that followed, long days, expensive days, in court, anxiety and suffering for several people.

Mr. Rankin took counsel's opinion and was reminded that he acted in Ulster as Solicitor for Minors, and he was advised to report the matter to the Lord Chief Justice, which he did. The case was then brought to court by another solicitor acting, in Mr. Rankin's place, as Solicitor for Minors; an injunction was sought to restrain the trustees from selling the shares. No one asked me for the simple explanation that could have cleared up the whole matter.

At the outset there was a strange line of argument as to what constituted the correct conduct of a business deal. It was stated that there must have been something wrong with this deal because I had bought from the minority shareholders at the same price as from the others. No one pointed out that this, in the view of the City of London, was the only proper way to purchase a company.

Counsel for the plaintiff (the Solicitor for Minors) also inferred that I was getting a bargain in these shares by having got at the two trustees. Apparently in order to induce them to sign the agreement with me, I had given them both new service contracts with increased salaries as executives of the *Telegraph* company.

This inference did not seem to recognize the simple facts nor was it fair to the two trustees. The contracts bound the two men to the firm for fifteen years for an extra £400 a year, which was not by any count a big deal for them, and besides that, with a new firm taking over and no trust shares for them to look after, the chances were that they would lose their directorships and the fees of £500 a year.

But Maurice Gibson Q.C. for the plaintiff could invite the judge to consider 'how to sell property worth over a million pounds. It is a very simple transaction. Mr. Thomson meets them and he says, "I will give you £20 a share"; and they say "Thank you very much" and they shake hands. And then Mr. Thomson says, "I will give you a service contract with me for fifteen years at an increased salary," and they say "Thank you very much indeed," and they then all have lunch together and they sign on the dotted line. But is that how trustees should exercise their diligence in getting a proper price for shares?'

As a matter of fact, after signing that agreement with the trustees and the widow, when I heard of Jeans's inspired offer of £21, I wired to McMaster an offer of £22. Subsequently my advisers said this was a great mistake. For it could then be asked in court why the trustees had been so willing to let the boy's shares go to me for £20 when, not long afterwards, I had been willing to pay £22.

Mr. Justice McVeigh was then to hear Mr. Gibson Q.C. say: 'It was a transaction which was conceived and plotted in secrecy, carried through by stealth and sought to be hidden from the world by deceit.'

This as I knew was a contradiction of the facts, as was subsequently admitted.

Finally, Mr. Justice McVeigh advised the parties to the case to seek a settlement on the basis that the shares would be sold to me at a price that would be fair to the minor. It was my understanding that the Lord Chief Justice, who had found himself in a very uncomfortable position once the facts were known, had advised the inclusion of this direction that the shares be sold to me, but in order to save his face that the price should be slightly increased.

I was several times tempted to wash my hands of the whole affair and let them see then what price they could get for the poor minor's shares. It would certainly have been less than my offer. But I had tied up a considerable amount of money in the matter and I had made an agreement and I could not back out of it. I refused however to add more than two shillings to my increased offer, making the price £22 2s.

As all this dragged on, it looked to us that the *Telegraph* was doing nothing else in the meantime but lose money. But we could not get R. M. Sayers to agree to permit us to participate in the operation, so in May we made a move in court and Mr. Justice McVeigh, recalling that he had directed the parties to do nothing to the detriment of the minor's property, accepted an agreement to reconstitute the Board, with our representation.

Jim Coltart became a director and went over to Belfast to look after the paper's commercial situation.

Finally, on 19th September, it was announced to Mr. Justice McVeigh that an agreement had been reached with me, and counsel stated that Maurice Gibson Q.C. had authorized him to state that Mr. Thomson's 'integrity and honour were in no way in question and that no suggestion had been made, or was ever intended, against his good name.'

That, after what had been said in court, was more than I could stomach. Such imputations of my integrity and honour as were made in Belfast have never been made in any other court or, so far as I know, in any other place. Though I own its main newspaper, and though I was invited on one occasion by the Governor General and again by the Prime Minister, I have never gone back to that tragic city. I never will.

This whole affair left me with a great feeling of unhappiness and a deep sense of injustice. The accusations they hurled at me, though later rescinded, were the one blot on my business career.

For the record, I should add that, even under the editorship of J. E. Sayers, whom we kept in office, and to a more substantial degree under that of Eugene Wason, who succeeded him, the *Belfast Telegraph* became a more liberal and fairer and a much better paper. Maybe this advance of liberalisation in the paper was really what had been fought in that court. And it was one of the changes that came too late to stop the Ulster tragedy.

Another blow that fell upon my head at this period of my life was over the moves for a merger with Odhams.

It was my habit still to offer to buy any newspaper which might come into any discussion, and one of the first 'bites' that came at this time, in fact before the Belfast case was settled, was a suggestion by Sir Christopher Chancellor of Reuters, just before he took over the chairmanship of Odhams, with that sprawling empire, that I should buy the Odhams newspapers and leave him the numerous magazines which Odhams ran with marked success.

I was not averse to working on this proposition, and I figured eventually that what would work would be a merger of the two companies, Odhams and mine. This would create the most comprehensive and powerful media group ever known, and it need fear no one. Why should we hold back from the concept simply because it was so big? Christopher Chancellor invited Jim Coltart and me to lunch with several of the directors of Odhams, but I got a surprisingly cool reception when I outlined my plan, and I was finally turned down flat.

Then, at a Christmas cocktail party given by Lord Rothermere, Sir Christopher, now chairman of Odhams, met Cecil King, chairman of the *Mirror* group. The situation in the women's magazine field had become worse. There were not enough readers or advertisers for all the magazines being published. Some of them had to go, either through suicidal competition or through some kind of agreement. And this was apparently Cecil King's greeting to Christopher, from one Wykehamist to another: 'Why do we go on battling with each other with the women's magazines? If you stop one of yours, I'll stop one of mine.'

Followed a lunch between them, with Christopher taking along his two directors, Charles Shard and H. L. Gibson, and the suggestion being made that Odhams should take over the Fleetway magazines (formerly Amalgamated Press) which belonged to the *Mirror* group. Never at a loss for a figure (and no doubt he had this all prepared) King said it would cost them £10m., and Odhams reckoned, though this hadn't been said, that they had been given a pretty firm offer, and that was the price, take it or leave it.

At a further meeting, this time in King's house, the Odham's men indicated that the proposition was too extensive for them; they would need to be assured that they would make £2m. profit if they paid £10m. for Fleetway. It wasn't on. King, by 20th January, 1961, then proposed a merger through an exchange of shares. Christopher Chancellor would be vice-chairman and seats on the board would be given to the two Odhams directors, Shard and Gibson. A merger would bring about sizeable savings and they could cut down and rationalize the women's magazines, which had bred too fast in the immediate post-war period. Taking him aside as they were leaving, Christopher asked King, old boys of the same school, if he was preparing a takeover bid, and, according to Christopher, King replied to this effect: 'I haven't reached that point yet. I am proposing a merger. But don't keep me waiting for your answer.'

Cecil King formalized his proposal in a letter to Christopher Chancellor of 24th January. But by then Christopher had been in touch with me again.

His story was that his daughter had attended a ball at which she had danced with an executive from a well-known merchant-banking firm, who had said to her, apparently in all innocence, 'I hear your father's going to have a new boss.' This was enough for Christopher. He phoned me that morning to arrange an immediate meeting. No one else could save him, now.

I am going into some detail in this chapter of recent history because few people who take part in these convulsive affairs ever get the chance, or take the trouble, to tell what goes on behind the scenes, and if they did I don't think they would reveal it as the unacceptable face of capitalism that some people think it is. But in this case Hugh Cudlipp, who was then Cecil King's right-hand man, wrote a book about it, *At Our Peril*, and I don't want my side of the battle, as he called it, to go under-represented.

Recognizing that Cecil King's remark to him, that he would not wait too long for a proposal, was a clear warning, Christopher Chancellor had not waited until the young man's remark at the ball threw him into determined action. He had already called in Odhams' financial advisers, N. M. Rothschild, and was told that the only defence against a *Mirror* takeover bid would be the sort of merger that I had proposed nearly a year before, and which Christopher Chancellor and his board had, perhaps too impetuously, turned down. The Odhams board discussed this on the morning of 23rd January, and by tea-time were in session with me.

These negotiations were as intensive as any I have taken part in and by eight o'clock on the evening of 25th January we had reached agreement. Kenneth Keith and Derek Palmar of Philip Hill, Higginson, Erlangers produced a scheme whereby Odhams would buy Thomsons and would pay me with 29 per cent of Odhams ordinary stock, which, though a good bit short of a majority holding, would still give me complete working control. A new company, Thomson-Odhams Ltd. (I insisted on the Thomson coming first) would be formed, and would, we felt sure, be too big for Cecil King to attempt to take over. I would be chairman and Sir Christopher would be vice-chairman, and three representatives from each company would form the board.

Christopher wrote to Cecil King saying that his board could see no advantage in such a merger as King had proposed. Moreover they had in mind an entirely different plan for their company, which in their view had much greater long-term advantages and prospects and which would give the company a degree of diversification and strength which would have lasting value. He then called a press and TV conference in the Connaught

Rooms for the following day, 26th January. King and his colleagues, who had not been given time to find out about our negotiations, were dumbfounded. What had happened to cause Chancellor's change of mind and new very firm tone?

The merger was announced as a fact at the press conference. From what I said, I was obviously sensitive about one aspect of our union that had nothing to do with Cecil King:

'Odhams are a big magazine business: Thomson has no magazines. Odhams have a bill-posting business: Thomson has no bill-posting. Odhams has a daily national newspaper. I think that we could say, as far as the Sunday newspapers are concerned, no one could claim that the *Sunday Times* and *The People* are competitors. We have television: Odhams have no television. We have a group of provincial newspapers: Odhams have no provincial newspapers. Now how can anyone claim that this is in any way creating a monopoly, or minimizing competition, or putting the control of any section of the press that had previously been divided into any one hand? It is just not possible.

'This was a natural marriage of convenience and everything in it fitted into this picture of grouping together for security, for putting both our companies together into a position of strength and development, without in any sense lessening competition.'

The *Daily Herald* next morning carried a statement by its editor, John Beavan, saying the newspaper had been 'saved'. But the *Financial Times* said it looked as if the stage had been set for a takeover battle. While in the House of Commons M.P.s debated my monopolistic tendencies and were promised a statement by the Prime Minister, Harold Macmillan, plans were being discussed by King and his directors for a bid for Odhams that would eliminate Thomson from the contest.

The bid was announced next morning, 28th January, in the *Daily Mirror*. For shares which, even after the Odhams-Thomson merger announcement had taken effect, were only forty shillings on the market, they now offered fifty-five shillings and three half-pence. This presented a considerable advantage to his shareholders, but Sir Christopher and his board said they could not recommend acceptance.

That day, Odhams organized a confidential meeting, luncheon in a private room at the Garrick Club, of all the parties who might be opposed to Cecil King's offer being accepted. Hugh Gaitskell, Labour Party leader, and George Brown attended, supposedly worried about the future of the *Daily Herald*, and George Woodcock of the T.U.C. was there with a similar role. Also present, besides Chancellor and myself, were the editors of the *Herald* and of *The People* (the latter of whom had some-what rashly described the Odhams takeover as an 'act of piracy'). Hugh Gaitskell did not favour the *Mirror* deal, but George Brown did not share his leader's doubts. The meeting had been called so that these two and George Woodcock could denounce the takeover, but they did not. It was obvious to me that whatever was said nothing would be done. Meanwhile, Hugh Cudlipp was writing to Gaitskell and King was writing to George Woodcock giving assurances in the event of the *Mirror* bid being successful. Cudlip published in the *Mirror* a guarantee that 'No amalgamation of the *Mirror* and the *Herald* will ever take place during the period of the *Mirror* group's control of Odhams.'

On Monday, 30th January, Cecil King and Cudlipp went to the House of Commons for a private lunch with Hugh Gaitksell and George Brown. The Labour men were quite plainly unhappy about the takeover and Gaitskell warned Cudlipp 'not to underestimate parlia-mentary feeling on the issue'. There could be no doubt,

Cudlipp wrote later, that feeling in the Labour Party was hostile to the *Mirror* attempt. And if the *Mirror* succeeded in its bid they were going to demand that Macmillan send it to a Monopolies Commission.

By Thursday, 2nd February, Cudlipp had got his colleagues to agree to giving an undertaking that the *Mirror* would run the *Herald* for a minimum period of seven years. He got on to Gaitskell but the latter was in Hampstead with a cold. George Brown went to inform the leader of the new guarantee and Frank Cousins declared himself now in favour of the *Mirror* offer.

Meanwhile, having no desire to enter into a battle for the Odhams shares at such a price, I decided to take myself off the stage. I have never, in all these years of acquiring businesses, entered into a takeover battle with another bidder, and I did not intend to start that game with a man like Cecil King as adversary. In any event Cecil King had everything to gain by buying Odhams, whereas I had only been tempted by receiving a good offer. I didn't need Odhams. So that I would not do anything that might queer whatever Christopher was planning, I went off to the Riviera without saying that I was giving up the fight.

I learned later that Cudlipp had me shadowed by the *Mirror* Riviera man and I imagine there must have been some head scratching when it was reported that my first call was upon Lord Rothermere. As a matter of fact, Rothermere and I never mentioned the *Mirror* bid for Odhams.

Odhams' directors then put out a statement that the bid was unacceptable. Meanwhile they had discussed possibilities with Sir William Carr of the *News of the World* and with Sir Eric Bowater of the newsprint company. Since the *Mirror* group were linked with Reed's, Bowater's biggest rival, Odhams were thinking that Sir Eric would like an alliance to ensure his sales. But he got it in fact from Cecil King who guaranteed an extended contract and thus eliminated Bowater's as a potential ally of Odhams.

The Odhams directors had a further meeting with the *Mirror* men but after talking for an hour 'mutually agreed to terminate the discussions'. The *Mirror* group then came out with an improved offer, raising the bid to 63s. a share against the market value at closing of 52s. That was 17th February and on 24th February the Odhams directors gave in. They issued to the shareholders a statement which included these paragraphs:

'Your directors have decided as individuals that they cannot accept the new *Daily Mirror* offer. Financially, however, the new offer to the ordinary stockholders is substantially better than the first. Your board cannot now advise you to refuse this improved offer.

'To clarify the position further, your directors have talked to Mr. Roy Thomson. As stated in the circular of 9th February your board sought with Thomson Newspapers an association in a form which was, in their view, in the long-term interest of the stockholders of the company. In the light of the changed circumstances Mr. Thomson has agreed at your board's request to cancel the arrangement.'

Though I reasoned with myself that there had been no great gain for me in merging with Odhams, I had none the less suffered a pretty severe disappointment. I had seen the glittering vista spreading out before me of being chairman of the new Thomson-Odhams Ltd. (even if it meant having only 39 per cent of the much bigger company) and then the very next day to have it all torn from my gaze was indeed a galling experience. So I tell myself. Yet I am being completely honest when I say I can't remember being particularly downcast. I do remember going to the reception given by Hugh Cudlipp, the *Mirror* managing director, to celebrate what he was pleased to call Cecil King's victory, and I don't think that took any effort on my part. Hugh was certainly surprised to see me walk into his celebration. All I wanted was to get on with something new.

I didn't realize at the time what a blessing it was that I had been kept out of Odhams. For there is no doubt, had that merger taken place, I would never have got *The Times*. They would never have offered it to me and if they had the Government would not have allowed me to take it. As to whether I would rather have had Odhams then or *The Times* later I don't think there is any possible doubt. And what would we have done with the *Daily Herald* and *The People*?

Confrontation that gave a first hint of détente: Khrushchev talks freely with Thomson on 9 February, 1962

Old friends: Lord Thomson paid a second visit in August 1964, and Khrushchev took him for a tour of the Virgin lands wheat-growing areas

Another breakthrough into the Communist world was the visit to Peking in 1972, when Lord Thomson and his party met Chou En-lai. In the lower picture Chou En-lai is flanked by Lord Thomson and the Hon. Kenneth Thomson with Mr George Rainbird behind.

A third Russian visit, in September 1965, to meet Chairman Kosygin

With President Tito on Brioni: discussion of a partnership in hotels

Photo Snowdon

Dinner to launch the *Sunday Times Business News*, April 1967, with Mr Harold Macmillan
Commonwealth Press Union Conference, June 1964, with the Prime Minister, Sir Alec Douglas-Home, and the Hon. Gavin Astor, C.P.U. Chairman

6

A JOB AT THE TOP

PERHAPS, SINCE apparently I had every intention of joining in big business, I had left it a little late in coming to London. I felt, in 1961, that I didn't have time to be patient. This was the period of the Odhams 'battle' and other big moves which followed it and I was then rising 67. You may take the view that age itself, and not only Cecil King, might have induced me to be a little more moderate in my ambitions. But—I have confessed this before—when I wasn't trying something new, seeking to enter into a new area of business, or making the moves for a new deal, I always had a restless feeling, a suspicion that I might be stagnating.

What pushed me on in 1961 was not really ambition at all. I would have said then, if anyone had asked me, that I had to keep going, it was my nature and there were other, practical, reasons. One, of course, was that, being a widower and my children all being settled with their own lives and families, if I retired I retired to loneliness, or else to being a nuisance, an incubus on a younger set of people with very different interests and habits, however warmly they would have welcomed me to their homes. That I never really considered. But it was being a widower that pushed me on and led to all that followed. Being a widower a man has to fill his life as best he can. I certainly seemed to fill mine pretty fully.

Of course I never really considered retiring. Life was too exciting. We were getting on too well. We knew by then, Jim Coltart and I, that our takeover of the Kemsley empire, which, privately, had daunted both of us at the start, was going to be a success. Going further back, I had felt a lot of misgivings, too, when in 1954, a 'shoe-string operator', as my Edinburgh banker called me, I took over the *Scotsman*, but these self-doubts had been resolved long ago; and since coming to London we had certainly made some giant strides. I knew by 1961 that in that newspaper business, highly sophisticated though it might be, we could hold our own; the opposition were by this time more likely to be apprehensive of us than we of them. As Jim recalls, there was a noticeable shift of attitude towards me even on the part of Lord Beaverbrook, who had been inclined to treat me as a roughneck from the backwoods.

Having said that, I must now ask myself: what was it that gave me this self-confidence, this determination and adventurous spirit in business . . . at 67?

It was at least partly due to my discovery over a fairly long period, but more than ever during these latter years in Edinburgh and London, that experience was a very important element in the management side of business and it was, of course, the one thing that I had plenty of. I could go further and say that for management to be good it generally must be experienced. To be good at anything at all requires a lot of practice, and to be really good at taking decisions you have to have plenty of practice at taking decisions. The more one is exposed to the necessity of making decisions, the better one's decision-making becomes.

At various times during my business life I have had to take some important decisions and, particularly in the early days, I often got these wrong. But I found later that the early mistakes and, for that matter, the early

104

correct decisions stood me in good stead. Most of the problems that I was confronted with in London were in one way or another related to those earlier ones. It was often a matter of just adding some zeros to figures and the sums were the same. In a great many instances I knew the answer immediately.

I cannot explain this scientifically, but I was entirely convinced that, through the years, in my brain as in a computer, I had stored details of the problems themselves, the decisions reached and the results obtained; everything was neatly filed away there for future use. Then, later, when a new problem arose, I would think it over and, if the answer was not immediately apparent, I would let it go for a while, and it was as if it went the rounds of the brain cells looking for guidance that could be retrieved, for by next morning, when I examined the problem again, more often than not the solution came up right away. That judgement seemed to be come to almost unconsciously, and my conviction is that during the time I was not consciously considering the problem, my sub-conscious had been turning it over and relating it to my memory; it had been held up to the light of the experi-ences I had had in past years, and the way through the difficulties became obvious. I am pretty sure other older men have had this same evidence of the brain's sub-conscious work.

This makes it all very easy, you may say. But, of course, it doesn't happen easily. That bank of experience from which I was able to draw in the later years was not easily funded.

The International Business Machines Company—one of the world's great business organisations—have had for many years a single word as their motto. A sign over every executive's desk spells it out: 'Think'. Let us be honest with ourselves and consider how averse we all are to doing just that. Thinking is work. In the early stages of a man's career it is very hard work. When a difficult decision or problem arises, how easy it is, after looking at it superficially, to give up thinking about it. It is easy to put it from one's mind. It is easy to decide that it is insoluble, or that something will turn up to help us. Sloppy and inconclusive thinking becomes a habit. The more one does it the more one is unfitted to think a problem through to a proper conclusion.

If I have any advice to pass on, as a successful man, it is this: if one wants to be successful, one must think; one must think until it hurts. One must worry a problem in one's mind until it seems there cannot be another aspect of it that hasn't been considered. Believe me, that is hard work and, from my close observation, I can say that there are few people indeed who are prepared to perform this arduous and tiring work. But let me go further and assure you of this: while, in the early stages, it is hard work and one must accept it as such, later one will find that it is not so difficult, the thinking apparatus has become trained; it is trained even to do some of the thinking subconsciously as I have shown. The pressure that one had to use on one's poor brain in the early stages no longer is necessary; the hard grind is rarely needed; one's mental computer arrives at decisions instantly or during a period when the brain seems to be resting. It is only the rare and most complex problems that require the hard toil of protracted mental effort.

I have called this a bank of experience which one builds up in one's early days and draws on heavily when one is older and perhaps beset by more problems. Certainly the sacrifice of one's pleasures in favour of hard work when one is young is very similar to the saving of money by sacrifice, by forgoing buying something that would give one a great deal of pleasure however short-lived. Those who save money calculate that the pleasure they will get later from the money saved will give them a greater or more lasting satisfaction (or a freedom from anxiety). The sacrifice of leisure and pleasure in favour of work when one is young does, I believe, pay the same dividends, and these dividends come mostly from the experience stored away in the brain. I realized very clearly in my 60s that a lot of the sacrifices I had made when a young man were paying off a hundredfold.

I am putting this all on tape in the hope that it may reach some young men of the sort that I was, and that they will know they are not wasting their precious youth. In 1968 I was asked to write an introduction to a new edition of Samuel Smiles' *Self Help*, a Victorian classic which today is apt to produce a horse-laugh in certain quarters, yet which contains a great deal of truth and extremely helpful advice, and I remember this line: 'The most important results are obtained not through genius and intellect, but through simple means and ordinary qualities.' I can vouch for that.

I wrote then: 'As one who employs large numbers of people in his concerns, I recognize the truth of the following:

"Modest merit is too apt to be inactive, or negligent, or uninstructed merit. Well matured and well disciplined talent is always sure of a market, provided it exerts itself; but it must not cower at home and expect to be sought for. There is a good deal of cant, too, about the success of forward and impudent men, while men of retiring worth are passed over with neglect. But it usually happens that those forward men have that valuable quality of promptness and activity without which worth is a mere inoperative property. A barking dog is often more useful than a sleeping lion." '

And on the same theme I went on:

'One passage in this book I am totally in agreement with. In fact I would apply it personally to my own life and career. "On the whole," Smiles writes, "it is not good that human nature should have the road of life made too easy. Better to be under the necessity of working hard and faring meanly, than to have everything done ready to hand and a pillow of down to repose upon. Indeed, to start in life with small means seems so necessary as a stimulus to work, that it may almost be set down as one of the conditions to success in life." '

In that year of 1961, after the Odhams project had fallen through, we took stock of our position and realized we were facing a different kind of problem than hitherto, and yet not unlike the situation, though on a different scale, that I had faced in Canada when the Depression engulfed us. Then, too, I had been thankful that I could spread my interests and my credit into several businesses; I managed to survive by gaining on one what I lost on the other. In 1961 it was Denis Hamilton who pointed out to us that Thomson Newspapers Ltd., though prospering, was in a vulnerable position. In the first place, 50 per cent of our profits were coming from the television company and that company was at the mercy of political change and indeed in danger of losing its licence at the end of the period. More than this, he argued, the whole company was based on advertising revenue. This made us wholly susceptible to the ups and downs of the economy and again vulnerable to political moves such as deliberate deflation and dearer money. It was unlikely, too, that we would be able to acquire any more newspapers without criticism of monopoly.

There was obviously a need for a diversification of our business, an urgent need, as had been contended. Our first efforts towards this end were not, however, entirely successful.

We proceeded in four fields. First, in publishing books.

To make the most of the big success that was coming to the *Sunday Times*, we made an agreement with *Time Life* in America to produce in association with them some of their beautifully illustrated and mainly educational books which we would sell by post in many countries as *Sunday Times* publications. The first, on Russia, was reasonably successful; the second, on Mexico, much less so. There had been, we discovered, a large and quite absurd miscalculation.

It arose through an executive, who came from *Readers' Digest* to work with us on the new project, being entirely unfamiliar with the way British newspapers are run. He believed that the *Sunday Times* would have lists of the names and addresses of their readers, as American papers did, many deliveries there being made by the post office as mail. It was on this belief that he had based all his projections of the new enterprise, and using the mail-shot technique of which he was thoroughly familiar, he saw us getting at the up-market readers of the *Sunday Times* and he could estimate how many we would sell, and whether any one book needed an extra 'shot' and so on. He couldn't fail. Unfortunately, no such lists were available and then there was nothing he could do but fail.

The second enterprise was in printing. We had acquired several commercial printing plants from Kemsley and we had taken over others in the publishing concerns we had bought since. Thomson Printers Ltd. was formed but after a while it became evident that it was not achieving the objectives we had set it and we were successful in selling a majority stake to the British Printing Corporation which had a great deal more experience in this business than we had.

The third branch of our expansion, which also failed to give us one of the new successful lines we were looking for, was in commercial and educational systems, speed-writing, language courses, and some time later, news-casters. These, too, had all to be disposed of; we were getting the classic answer, which we were slow to accept, of the cobbler and his last. In spite of these set-backs we remained convinced that there had been such a build-up of skills in the organisation that we must not and could not fail to employ them successfully in other fields.

In the fourth concern, we had been in fact highly successful. That was in periodical publishing where, at first, we concentrated on specialist and trade papers and magazines. In this case we acquired new executives with the skills and experience to exploit this new field and the Thomson Organisation offered them the scope to develop their ideas and their talents.

Gordon Brunton had rejoined Odhams in January 1961, as personal assistant to the Managing Director and with a view to succeeding him; he had been given a seat on the executive board by Sir Christopher Chancellor. When Odhams were taken over by the *Mirror* group, Sir Christopher came to see us in Gray's Inn Road. He believed he had some apologizing to do over the way the takeover 'battle' had gone. Whether that was so, or not, what was more important to us was his recommendation of the young man in Odhams whom they had been grooming for the top job. We might have been unlucky to lose Odhams, Christopher said, but we shouldn't lose this young man.

I rang that day to Odhams but I missed him. I had then to leave for Canada, and by the time I returned I dare say I didn't remember anything about him. But I had worked out a pretty meticulous system. My staff had been trained to produce for me, on my return from any visit, a list of every single person who had called when I was away and what they had wanted. So I saw that one Gordon Brunton had returned my call and beside his name the word 'Odhams'. I still wasn't sure what that portended, but I took a chance and spoke to him and asked him if he would come over and talk to me about the publishing business.

He did, and after ten minutes—it wasn't any more—I, of course, had recalled Christopher Chancellor's words and I had also swiftly concluded that they were well justified. I asked Gordon if he would join me. I recall telling him, 'I don't think I'll be tempting you with money, but what I can offer you is opportunity.' This Gordon saw, fortunately. He must have seen that what we did with our money was to go wide and far, to hunt out opportunities for expansion, to enjoy the real freedom of enterprise. So he joined us, and he very soon brought others, like Geoffrey Parrack and Tim Hedgecock, to help us, and there never was any doubt about our spirit of enterprise.

In one year, from the latter part of 1961, Thomson Publications achieved a very remarkable growth. This was the company of which, from its incorporation, Gordon Brunton took charge. In 1961 he had taken over a group of trade and technical papers operating in South Africa, to be followed over the coming months with printing and publishing interests in Salisbury, Southern Rhodesia, and Malawi. This was followed by the acquisition of Illustrated Newspapers Ltd., a fine publishing group publishing *Illustrated London News*, *Tatler*, and two very important trade papers, *Men's Wear* and *Draper's Record*. With Illustrated Newspapers came the great book publishing house of Michael Joseph. Illustrated Newspapers also owned a group of printing plants, mainly in London.

Illustrated Newspapers was a really big deal, which came to us largely because Sir John Ellerman, who owned the controlling interest in the company, had been one of the stockholders of Odhams who had sold out to Cecil King, and he believed that defeat in that tussle had hurt me. Sir John was a very shy man, who didn't expose himself very readily to new acquaintances. I was touched —and indeed flattered—when he had me to dinner with himself and his wife, no doubt to convince himself that I was the right sort to take over the business. In fact we got a very good deal and were able subsequently to sell off the Illustrated printing businesses so neatly that they almost paid for all the other properties.

Our start in taking control of the firm of Michael Joseph wasn't altogether promising, however. I'm afraid I did not then know very much about book publishers. When I met the three directors I began to talk about the revolution that was already overdue and badly needed in the old-fashioned ways of British publishers, about which I thought everyone agreed, and how they would benefit from the application of our marketing skills and so on. All fairly ordinary stuff. But all three directors, Charles Pick, Roland Gant and Peter Hebdon, sent in their resignations next morning. I was to learn that book publishing was a highly individual business, each publishing house having its own style and owing much to the personality and impulses of the chairman, or the men who ran it, and the whole industry had long defied attempts to rationalize it.

In this emergency Gordon called in Denis Hamilton and they persuaded Desmond Flower to become chairman of Michael Joseph's, and in the event Peter Hebdon rejoined the company. But for a day or two the chances of saving the firm we had just bought looked distinctly marginal, when we had a publishing house with one of the great imprints in fiction and three of the senior directors had resigned. Later we bought Thomas Nelson and Denis brought another famous imprint, Hamish Hamilton, to us.

About this time we got another, small group of trade papers. They were bought, I remember, from a widow, who when we approached her had taken financial advice, and she told Gordon the figure her advisers had put upon her business. Gordon came to me immediately and told me her business was worth a good deal more than she was asking. He wanted me to agree to offer her a higher price. I agreed without hesitation. It had always been our policy to offer what we genuinely believed a newspaper was worth to us, and the same principle must apply to a group of periodicals. When we were keen to take a paper over, our practice was to have a good look at the books, and there was no one better at taking a good look at books than I was, and then estimate how much more circulation we could obtain and how much that would mean in advertising revenue, and then have our boys look at the plant and estimate what we would need to spend, if anything, on modernizing it; putting all these factors together we arrived at a fair price and stuck to it; if anyone wanted to outbid us, let him. This was the procedure Jim and I had followed on numerous occasions, with the clear object of both seller and buyer being satisfied. It was how we had set to work in Belfast, before all the legal trouble started. So now Gordon went back to the widow and startled her with the news that our offer was going to be sizeably greater than what she had been asking. The upshot was that, before the deal was completed, when she received an offer from another quarter that exceeded ours, she turned it down and sold to us because, she said, we had been so straight with her.

A woman with an acute business brain, a Mrs. Meagan, provided us with a very similar experience. She was the owner of *Labour News*, which we turned into *Construction News* and it became the most successful of all our trade papers. She wanted a very high price for her property, and if we didn't like it, we could lump it. But Gordon was convinced it was a paper with great development potential and we agreed to her price. Just before completion, someone else came on the scene with a higher offer, but Mrs. Meagan kept her bargain with us because in the first place we hadn't tried to haggle with her.

We had been given fair warning about the need for diversification and in Thomson Publications we did not appear to waste any time about it. Having acquired, in conjunction with Colonel Harold Hemming, *Glass's Guide* which is the handbook of the second-hand car business, and which got us into what we call the service industry, we saw Gordon off to Australia to have a look at some trade and technical periodicals. I remember he came to see me before leaving.

'How do you want me to handle it?' He was still a new boy after all. 'Would you like a survey by telex or wait till I get back and report to you?'

'You will find half a million available at the bank,' I said. 'If you see anything worth buying, buy it.'

This was the way I invariably trusted my executives. I believed they could do most things as well as I could, if not better, and I always avoided the mistake of kidding myself to the contrary. Reverting again to good old Samuel Smiles, I see that in my preface, I drew attention to the fact that he lived in a world of one-man businesses and partnerships and because of this his list of business virtues missed out on this one essential quality that I myself, from long experience, reckon invaluable. A man must not only know how to choose his executives, he must know how to delegate authority. Lack of this ability shows not only a lack of trust in the individuals themselves but a failure to trust and back one's own judgement. Many of the business failures I have known about throughout my life have come about through this. A man who cannot delegate to others finds himself without the time or energy to concentrate on essential problems. Nor will he be able to take the kind of decisions that are active, immediate and effective. I had also found that it paid to give an executive that confidence right at the start of his career with me.

Gordon was quickly successful in Australia, and bought for us a group of the right kind of periodicals. And I recall that two days after he got back, I had him on the plane with me bound for Edinburgh and another deal, and the two of us arguing all the way north about how we should handle it. We were going to make an offer to Thomas Nelson and Sons, no less, to take over their considerable business in educational and other books. Gordon and I were arguing all the way to Turnhouse, and from the airport all the way by car to Selkirk, where we were to meet Nelson's chairman at his house. Our argument was on the point of whether the business was worth its valuation of assets or its valuation of earning power. When we stepped out of the car, and not until then, I told Gordon we would play it his way and base our offer on earnings.

In a remarkably short time we had bought the famous business—and in doing so on the basis Gordon had argued for, we had saved ourselves roughly £600,000.

'Now we will have a good dinner,' I said as we drove towards Edinburgh. 'Do you like spaghetti?'

I can imagine what he expected, but I took him to a café of my earlier acquaintance, and we had soup, spaghetti, and tinned fruit salad, for which Gordon now reminds me he paid the bill of 11s. 4d. It wasn't until I was just getting into bed, having arranged for an early call so that we could skip the hotel breakfast and catch the first flight to London, that I let my thoughts wander to stamp duty. On a purchase like this of Nelson's stamp duty would be sizeable. I couldn't get it out of my mind and for once wasn't able to sleep. When we met in the morning I told Gordon about it and when we got on the plane we were able to take only some coffee because we had the balance sheets and accounts spread out in front of us as we anxiously calculated the situation. By capitalizing some of the assets, we could reduce the stamp duty payable, we finally decided, from £30,000 to £20,000. I was satisfied.

I don't know exactly what Gordon thought of that trip, or what he thinks of it now, although he makes occasional oblique references to it, and how he was done out of a slap-up dinner and then his breakfast, but I think he learned a lot from it. About me, anyway. About how I am always open to be persuaded.

That was indeed a period of pretty considerable activity, a very exciting period for me and for my directors, and the details I have given of it do not include the numerous abortive negotiations, nor the considerable research that we had, of course, to do before we went into these new businesses, new fields. Within the space of twelve calendar months we had secured a foothold in the consumer, trade and technical magazine markets, and had acquired very reasonable examples of the different types of periodicals that were being produced for these markets. We were also established in both general and educational publishing, at a high level of both.

I was happy. My top men were happy, feeling the thrust and spread of the exciting business they were now running. In spite of some failures, we had broadened our base, and we had made good use of the profits that were flowing in from television. One thing I could never abide was the leaving of money to lie idle, or even to have credit and not use it.

I was happy because I was getting plenty of budgets and balance sheets to keep me busy. With my eye on these figures, the individual operations of each firm in our increasing spawn of companies were under constant surveillance. Since my early Canadian days we had worked out a system of cost accounting and budgeting that was applied to all our activities, even to the editorial side of newspapers. I was able to tell from the monthly summary of revenue and expenditure of the biggest or smallest concern in the organisation, with a quick reference to the budget comparison, how things were going and to spot if anything looked wrong.

In almost all businesses, the revenue fluctuates by months and seasons of the year. In most cases costs have a relationship to the sales of that particular time, but many costs are fixed and cannot readily be changed to conform with a monthly change of revenue. Our budgets are all set up on the basis of average monthly costs for the whole year, and then every month is separately budgeted for revenue, so that the fluctuations don't make any one month look better or worse than it really is, and we also show each month what we've got to do during the remainder of that year.

Every year I always spent some of the summer months and then Christmas-time in Canada, and on my winter visit I always worked with St. Clair McCabe and Miss Hamilton on the final drafts of their budgets, just as I had done in Britain in November and early December before leaving. These budgets had been set up during the previous two months by the top men of all our various businesses all over the world, who had then gone into head office to argue them with the General Manager or Managing Director of the region or country. All these men in their responsible way had gone over every single cost and determined in the light of their sales experience what their expenditure should be. It was a great spreading complex of items and totals, pluses and minuses, risks and adventures, victories and failures, and yet to one pair of eyes in Toronto, as in London, it all made sense, it all came together in a pattern of activities, diverse and individual, and yet, when I took hold of it like that, a controlled and viable whole.

They tried to tell me in Britain that budgets did not really work with newspapers; editorial costs, for instance, were bound to fluctuate wildly, and sometimes could not be kept within pre-fixed limits. But I showed them that you could start with a wide margin, you would get more accuracy as the years passed, and that budgets would be a particular help to editors. The Economist Intelligence Unit, when it carried out its report on the press, was much impressed with our budgeting, and recommended other papers to follow our example.

One of the great advantages of budgets is that to achieve something near to accuracy of forecasting, one must completely analyse the details of costs. It is remarkable then what you find out when you set down on paper what your costs are for every single item necessary in the operation of the company. Managers have often told me that they had never known the real facts—or all the facts—about their operation until they looked into their expenses in preparing a budget. In this activity many extravagances are uncovered and many opportunities to effect savings which can be used elsewhere are brought to light. Unless costs and revenues are predetermined and set down so that from one month to another the results are always being brought as near as can be to the estimates, a balanced judgement will not be brought to bear on the operations. And it is just as important to inquire why one figure happens to be so far below the budget of costs as why another figure is so far above it.

I recall in my first year at Gray's Inn Road, I was told in passing by one of my directors that he was coming well inside his budget expenditure. 'That can't be good budgeting,' I told him. 'Or maybe you've been skimping.'

When one operates a number of businesses, it is astonishing how somewhere along the line one finds one manager or other who seems to have had a mental

118

blackout. He has done things and incurred costs well out of line with what was necessary or sensible. This would be happening to us all the time if every manager did not have before him a complete budget of what he was expected to do. That budget was always so comprehensive that it would leave no scope for the manager to make any seriously wrong decisions because they would not fit into his figures. Where conditions changed and seemed to be outside his control, our manager knew he had to get in touch with head office, to discuss the changes and to bring into play our experience and our expertise.

In addition to budgeting our revenue and costs, we also budgeted our cash flow for the year and carefully estimated what the cash position would be each month during the year. This enabled us to plan ahead for bank loans and possible debenture issues. Before we did this, we occasionally found ourselves in a tight financial position owing to certain circumstances not envisaged in the budget, such as making the purchase of a new business, which was often expedient though one didn't have the cash or the credit to cover it. That sometimes resulted in opportunities being lost, and that surely is tempting fortune.

Not everyone seemed to understand my love of budgets and balance sheets. They didn't seem to comprehend that, simply by checking figures, I could share in the guidance and excitement of a great number of operations, sometimes at the distance of an ocean or a continent. What I was watching was the flow of cash from one part of the organisation to another, testing it as if it were oil or life-blood, gauging that one area or section was not being starved of it, another part was not being overfed.

Believe me, this was a fascinating job. It was also an essential one. This was why I let my executive directors get on with the running of the organisation, and kept myself clear of their every-day affairs. This, above all, was why I didn't retire when I was sixty-five. I had a job to do. And, for my money, I didn't believe that anyone could do it any better.

7

INDEPENDENT VOICES

IN THAT same year of 1961, when we came so near to merging with Odhams and all their magazines, we announced that we were going to start a magazine of our own; it would come out as part of the *Sunday Times*. This, of course, had nothing to do with our failure to join with Odhams, though it was an effective answer to anyone who believed we were dejected over that affair. We were starting on many new lines that surprised our competitors (and detractors) and which we would not have been able to tackle if we had gone in with Odhams.

The first of these innovations was the colour magazine that was to be produced as a giveaway addition to the *Sunday Times*, which was at this time beginning to boom. Our first idea had been to add it to the Friday editions of our evening papers; but these did not have a large enough up-market circulation to enable us to charge a high enough advertising rate to cover our costs. After that our calculation was that the *Sunday Times* had reached, or would shortly reach, a circulation that was near to optimum, and possibly the only size—and kind— of circulation that could feasibly support a giveaway colour magazine; that is to say, its up-market sale would command a revenue from advertisers that would pay for its costly production at Watford.

This was an entirely new undertaking in Britain and one that was greatly to change the outlook of the quality

Sunday papers. We didn't believe that a paper like the *Sunday Express*, with a circulation around four million, and a relatively low advertising rate, could ever hope to pay for the printing of a magazine which had no cover price. In fact our figures showed that the more advertising they got and the more pages they needed, the more money it would lose. There was, in any case, no photogravure printing capacity in the country to cope with such a big circulation. This meant that we would have the position of market leader, at least, and apart from attracting many new readers to the *Sunday Times* it might, at the advertising rate which we would be able to charge for our quality readership, even make money.

It was Lord Beaverbrook who felt that our colour magazine thwarted his ambition to be the first to put colour into his newspapers. I felt that the inclusion of a colour magazine on glossy paper, still as part of the newspaper, was the only way at that time to accomplish this.

I always had great faith in the *Sunday Times Magazine* and a personal affection for it. It was my brain-child and it robbed my executives of all peace until it got off the ground. I had great hopes for it, and in the first 18 months those hopes cost me £900,000. That is a lot of money to pour out on a slim little giveaway, which was supposed to follow on American lines but didn't.

It has also been thoroughly capable of creating its own sensations. The first, in fact, was scarcely a week after the magazine started in January 1962. Without having given a hint of anything like that being in the wind, Denis Hamilton, then Editor of the *Sunday Times* as well as editorial director of the group, announced that he had engaged Lord Snowdon, whose talents were not perhaps so well recognized then as they are today, to be artistic adviser to the new magazine and that Lord Snowdon would also on occasions do work for it as a photographer.

The gossip over this appointment of Princess Margaret's husband, and the interest in it of other papers, was fairly intense, but Lord Snowdon was able soon enough to attend office conferences and to go out on photographic assignments without being followed by other photographers trying to take *his* picture. This was what he dearly wanted to do, to fit something of a professional career into the pattern of royal engagements which his marriage obliged him to keep, and it is what he went on to do with notable success.

I didn't escape from some involvement in this affair. Here, from the transcript, is John Freeman cross-examining me on the BBC *Face to Face* programme:

J.F. Did the editor of the *Sunday Times* consult you and ask your permission before he appointed Lord Snowdon to his job?

R.T. He told me about it, yes.

J.F. Well, did he consult you? Did he ask your permission?

R.T. He didn't need to ask my permission. He has *carte blanche* to engage anyone he thinks will improve the paper, but he told me about it, and, of course, I was aware of what was going on.

J.F. The idea was his and not yours?

R.T. The idea was his.

J.F. Did you have any doubts at all about the propriety of it?

R.T. Never.

J.F. You didn't feel you had any responsibility to anyone outside of the organisation?

R.T. No, I don't think there's any responsibility at all.

J.F. Were you confident when you thought about it that this very capable photographer really had the experience to do the highly technical job in magazine artwork which he is now being used for?

R.T. I don't think his qualities are confined to being a photographer. He's a very talented young man. He's the type of young man we are anxious to have in our business. And I have no question at all that he has the capabilities that we require.

J.F. I'm sure that he is a very capable young man. So are lots of unemployed journalists. The point is that his experience has never gone as far as this before, has it?

R.T. I don't know of any other unemployed journalist that has his qualities.

J.F. Are you satisfied, or were you satisfied at the time when your editor had this bright idea, that it wasn't just a publicity stunt?

R.T. Oh, I'm quite satisfied.

J.F. If you'd had to pay for the publicity you got as a result of this appointment, well I suppose you would agree that, whatever Lord Snowdon's salary may be, it's been paid a hundred times over. You'd agree with that, wouldn't you?

R.T. I'll agree that we've had a lot of publicity.

J.F. The colour magazine of the *Sunday Times*, if I may say so, shows every sign of needing an artistic adviser, and it would be difficult to imagine a more attractive inducement to the advertiser than Lord Snowdon?

R.T. I don't think that's the truth at all. I think they're going to buy the colour magazine on its quality. And I agree with you. I'm disappointed with the first issue, but if you see the second or the third you'll see a tremendous improvement.

Incidentally when I look back at that first issue I can now see what objective the *Sunday Times* staff had in mind. Denis Hamilton was anxious not only to attract a quarter of a million new readers but he wanted them all in the under-35 age-group, who would be ready for new journalistic treatment, and, of course, they would be an attraction to the advertisers once the latter realized that many *Sunday Times* readers were of an age to spend money on building up their homes.

Yet in spite of this completely successful editorial effort—it put up the circulation of the paper by nearly 200,000 in the first year—the advertising agencies continued to look at our new creation with some disdain and chose largely to ignore it. I cannot understand why they were so indifferent to it.

We struggled on for a year without the kind of support from advertisers that we should have had. As we approached the magazine's first birthday, there was a strong and persistent rumour that we were going to close it down. This worried us. In the brief and uncertain life of a colour magazine, of which species so many had died the death in Britain that they became at one time virtually extinct, nothing could have done more harm than a persistent rumour like that. Nothing could have been *calculated* to do more harm.

I have always believed that I knew who was making that calculation and instigating that rumour. He was during his life a man for whose prowess in the newspaper world and for whose abilities I never lost the greatest respect, not even after this malicious attempt to stifle our brilliant creation. For it was no less than that. In colour magazine publishing, you have to make your arrangements many months in advance, and if agencies believed that among the long-term allocations they made there might be one that would have to be cancelled, they were inclined not to make that allocation and so avoid trouble for themselves and their clients.

To convince these people that we were going up rather than down, we had to do something spectacular. They surely would treat anything we told them with pronounced scepticism. We couldn't hope that they would

125

believe that it was the inclusion of the magazine with the *Sunday Times* that had put up the circulation of the paper by nearly two hundred thousand, though that, indeed, happened to be true.

We had by this time a creative department. That was what it called itself. It was intended to handle a situation like this. Go to it, we said. Before any of us could grasp what was happening, the storm troops had gone to Intourist and the Russian Embassy and we were chartering a big Russian jet. To celebrate the birthday of the *Sunday Times Magazine*, we were going to fly 168 leading British businessmen as our guests for a few days in Moscow—the first such plane-load that had ever flown over the frozen steppes. It wasn't as easy to set up a jaunt like that as it is to tell you about it, but that was one of the modern skills we had taken on with a marketing department. None the less it was a remarkable achievement, for we were then at a very cold period of the cold war, and the chance of deals between our businessmen and the Russian trade officials was a slim one.

As it happened, our Moscow picnic engendered far more publicity for the magazine than we could have dreamed of. After meeting Alexei Adzhubei, editor of *Izvestia*, and a group of Russian industrial chiefs at a lunch, I received an invitation to the Kremlin to meet and talk with Adzhubei's father-in-law, Mr. Khrushchev.

This suddenly arranged meeting must have been decided upon for much wider and important reasons than because Adzhubei thought Khrushchev would find me amusing. Khrushchev wanted to talk to me because I was a leading newspaper publisher of the West and he wanted to say something to the West. When he received me in the Kremlin, and with me my son, Ken, two of my directors, Eric Cheadle and Michael Renshaw, and a *Sunday Times* man, Tom Stacey, he very soon embarked on a talk with me that was serious, wide-ranging, hard-hitting and enjoyable. It lasted all of two and a half hours and it became a big news story.

When we got back to the hotel, we found all the Western correspondents in Moscow waiting for us. They had recognized that in his willingness to see us and in his readiness to talk so freely, Khrushchev seemed to be signifying the beginning of a thaw in the cold war, of a desire for a *détente*. When we came to London Airport on our return we were met by pressmen in their full force from practically every country in the world. As the story could not properly be told without explaining how and why the trip to Moscow had been organised and who had organized it, a reference to the *Sunday Times Magazine* appeared in nearly every edition of the world's press. It must have seemed then to the advertising men in London that, for a one-year-old, it was very far from being closed down.

Its financial success was never in doubt from that day. Soon, other newspapers, which had freely and publicly scoffed at our innovation, now felt obliged to follow it with less likelihood of making a profit.

This success was a thrill for me. Who wouldn't be glad to have such a brain-child? Like many modern fathers, I had at the same time to admit to being slightly bewildered. It was like having a son you hoped was going to play for Arsenal when he grew up and then you found him studying abstract sculpture at Hornsey College of Art. The magazine was a strong, wilful and wayward child, and what he got up to, like most parents I freely confess I didn't always appreciate or even approve. I loved it but I didn't always understand it. If I had once thought that the product that finally made the grade in England would bear the slightest resemblance to the things we published in North America, I was never more wrong. Like all children, this one didn't turn out as its parent had hoped. It turned out better.

By some enterprise and because of a certain degree of good fortune, we were in the right place at the right time to try and do something new in British journalism. It cost us much heartache and much money and it cost some of my executives some headaches, but in the end a new idea was born and was realized. The *Sunday Times Magazine*, and its imitators, have undoubtedly become a feature of British life. It was, in the second year of its life, a formidable success; it became easily the leading magazine for photo-journalism in the world, outclassing anything similar in North America or elsewhere. It flew teams of writers and photographers, and often executives, too, to all parts of the world where the action was, it did more than just complement the *Sunday Times* newspaper, and it produced some of the best photo-reporting that I (and some less biased judges) had ever seen.

The great advantage the new magazine got from me, I would say now, as much perhaps as that solid financial backing for a patient start, was its independence. This all our papers had and, of course, still have. I gave our editors without exception complete independence in their editorial opinions; I not only said that this was my policy but I made sure that everyone could see that it was.

This we did in all our papers, on both sides of the Atlantic. If we couldn't pick the right editor for the best decision-making in each locality, then we should give the job to someone else. This was a theme to which I often returned in those days, as I went on making speeches and being questioned on TV and radio (I never ducked a chance to bring publicity to our papers). I see from the transcript that this is what I said on BBC's *Press Conference*:

THOMSON: I delegate completely to editors and local managers the authority to determine their own editorial content. In that respect I think I am rather unique.

128

WILLIAMS (Lord Francis-Williams): But supposing you find one of your editors is following an editorial policy which, for the time being, is unpopular—as many great editors have on occasion in the past—would you still give him freedom? Or is your freedom conditioned within a budget?

THOMSON: It's conditioned within a budget because it is a business enterprise and I can only allot the editor the reasonable amount of money based on the intake the paper will have. But I would certainly carry along with him, if I felt that he was sincere in what he was doing, and if his views were sound. Now if one of our editors became insincere or sensational or destructive, I'd have to do something about it. I think you'd agree that it would be my responsibility. But that's largely theory, because it has never happened in my experience. I'm careful of the top men that I pick.

WATERHOUSE (Keith Waterhouse): Can we take an example on this? You own papers in the southern United States, and you will be owning papers in Nigeria. It's conceivable that the American papers would be in favour of segregation, and it's likely, of course, that the Nigerian papers would be against it. Would you interfere with either?

THOMSON: Neither. The editors and the managers, as I have said, and I repeat, are absolutely in charge of the editorial policy of the paper, and I would not interfere. How could I in London intelligently interfere out there? Even on a thing like segregation—now I don't believe in segregation, and I don't believe most decent people do believe in it—but at the same time, if you're living in the Southern States and everybody in the community believes in it, how can I be sure that in that area, at that moment, it isn't the right answer?

This independence of editors was something I believed

129

in profoundly; it wasn't just a sales gimmick. It had begun in Canada when we were a small concern, and I had a statement of my policy printed on a card. It had grown deeper in my philosophy as I grew bigger in the media business, and still I refused to believe that I knew as well as the editors what was best, editorially. Apart from being the way that produced the best and most honest newspapers, it was the only sensible way for a man to run as many newspapers as I owned.

I remember very clearly an incident in Canada, when I bought a paper in Port Arthur, Ontario. The editor was in Toronto on holiday at the time, and the proprietors telephoned him there so that he would not be left to learn what had happened by reading the morning paper. Next morning at nine o'clock he was calling on me and having a very pleasant chat with his new owner. Then, 'Before I leave,' he said, 'what are my instructions?'

This being the first time we had met, I stared at him for a moment, not comprehending. 'I haven't thought about any instructions,' I said then. 'But yes, I have some. You go back and run that paper in the best interests of the people of Port Arthur. It is their newspaper. I will collect the revenues but it is their newspaper as far as the editorial contents are concerned. Your job is to support their interests above everything and everybody else, including me. I can look after myself. You look after them.'

As the years went on I became more and more convinced that this was right. A newspaper had a duty to represent and promote the best interests of the community—or the country—it served, and that didn't just mean echoing the majority opinion; although, if I had had a paper in a mining area, say, and it had been voicing distinctly right-wing opinions, I think I would have felt obliged to take a trip out to have a closer look at its editor to see if he were really suitable.

I had also developed ideas as to the role of the proprietor or managing director, both of whom, without
ever interfering with the editor's prerogative, had a
great deal to do with the success of a newspaper, great or
small.

All this recalls an incident on the *Scotsman*, which Jim
Coltart reminds me of, it being the first time he had
witnessed the effect of my policy on a newspaper and its
editor. At that time I had begun a rather friendly relationship with Anthony Eden, who was under fire for his
handling of Suez, and at lunch in the office one day I said
to the *Scotsman* editor, Alastair Dunnett: 'Don't be too
rough on Anthony. He gets a lot of criticism, more than
he deserves.' Next morning there was a blistering attack
on Eden in the *Scotsman*, but I never mentioned it.

It applied right across the board. This kind of principle,
if a man believes in it, he can't say it applies here or in
this connection, but not there or in that sort of affair.
Like peace, it is indivisible. It was the rigid rule that
governed the *Sunday Times*, too, and in this the difference
between the present and the previous ownership was
at its most striking. I recall how the *Sunday Times* was
for a period in 1963 critical of Harold Macmillan's
policies, and at this time I suspected that I was being
considered for an honour by the Prime Minister's committee. I had made no secret of the fact that I aspired
to a title one day. To me, the barber's son from
Timmins, the up-and-coming newspaper man who had
for so long admired the career of Lord Beaverbrook, the
wish for an honour from the British Prime Minister and
the Queen in my later days was a natural enough aspira-
tion, or so it seemed to me, and there was no guile in it.
Yet, as he took issue with the Conservative Government
on several occasions, the editor of the *Sunday Times*
never heard a word of reproach from me; I would have
bitten my tongue first.

It was a principle that went beyond a simple philosophic attitude. I just did not believe that newspapers were run properly, or can be run properly, if their editors are not given complete freedom. I did not believe that a newspaper was run efficiently, never mind properly, considering its circulation and its advertising revenues and the amount of capital invested in it, unless its editorial columns were run freely and independently by a highly skilled and dedicated professional journalist. If I show signs in my old age of interfering with the conduct of any of my newspapers in the way that the old press lords, Northcliffe, Rothermere, Beaverbrook and Kemsley, not to speak of Camrose, Southgate and Iliffe, did in the past, then I hope my son will stop me. He has been briefed to do this.

My attitude, though to me instinctive and perfectly natural, was a new one in the conduct of British newspapers, which had always been dominated by their proprietors, nearly all of whom, as you can see, had become lords. Such domination is not much in evidence nowadays. In this respect, I would say that the whole newspaper world here in Britain has changed radically. If I think this is partly due to the influence of my example, I must be excused for pride. If I introduced a new way of doing things, and new principles among the men who served the press, that was because I could not have done anything else, not without a great and worthless effort.

Mr. Macmillan was taken ill in October, 1963, but apparently from his sick bed, after he had handed over the Prime Ministership to Sir Alec Douglas-Home, he dictated a memorandum saying he would like my name to be included in the list of hereditary baronies in the New Year honours of 1964.

At that time I discovered to my surprise that in one respect I had done better than those other press chiefs who had been honoured before me—I was apparently the first of that ilk to think of using in my title the name of the Fleet River, which flows underground somewhere near Thomson House and Gray's Inn Road and then goes on its way to Fleet Street and the Thames. When I gave an 85th-birthday dinner to Lord Beaverbrook the following year he commented, in his brilliant speech, that I had stolen a march on all the previous Fleet Street barons who could have included Fleet in their titles and very likely hadn't thought of it.

8

MEN IN POWER

MR. KHRUSHCHEV never knew how he had helped us to bring off such a capitalistic success with the *Sunday Times Magazine*. At least I don't think he did: one couldn't make any such simple assumptions with that man. I certainly didn't tell him about it. Yet I feel sure that if he had known what his talk with us had done for the Magazine, he wouldn't have grudged us that help. It may seem strange to say this, but, in spite of the immense barriers of language, interpreters and protocol and the background of history, Khrushchev was a man with whom one felt almost at once on friendly terms; words might not be spoken but the sense of frankness and intimacy was there. During this period I met several of the men in power in the communist countries, and I got on better with Khrushchev than with any of the others, even if he did at times lose his cool with me. Whatever his political ideas, he was a man who had the instincts and the human warmth to make immediate contact with a stranger like myself.

I remember how he greeted me in his room at the Kremlin at our first meeting. 'Now you have to listen to what I say, Mr. Thomson,' he began. 'Remember I am your senior by two months.' This, of course, I discovered to be accurate: he had been born in April of the year 1894 when I appeared in June. And he had taken the trouble to find this out.

He invited me to visit him again two years after that publicity trip to Moscow, and this time, in August, 1964, he asked me if I would like to go with him on his train for a tour of Kazakhstan. Mr. Khrushchev quite clearly wanted to show me the success of the Russian harvest that year, or he simply wanted to enjoy seeing it himself, and my visit fitted in with that programme. In his very comfortable and well supplied private train we travelled into the Virgin Lands almost to the Caspian Sea, very often alone together, with or without an interpreter, as the train rolled across the tundra through mile after mile of golden wheat.

But, having been for a brief period of my life a farmer in Saskatchewan, I knew a bit about wheat-growing. I saw that that region which Khrushchev was showing me was not usually good wheat-growing land; it was too dry. The crop happened to be particularly good that year when they had had more rain than usual. But wait for twelve months, I thought: rain or no rain, I wouldn't count on seeing such beaming faces at the next harvest.

I knew what the trouble very likely was. Khrushchev had too many mouths to feed. The demand for wheat to be rushed from the collectives to the great industrial complexes and into the bread baskets of the cities was so great that they could not allow their farmers to maintain the 'summer fallowing' routine. Maybe it had been Khrushchev himself who had ordered the extent of that year's crop in Kazakhstan, and if so, no wonder he was pleased to see and to show me the results.

The 'summer fallowing' routine was how we had worked in Western Canada: cropping our wheat 'one year good' and then planting 'on the stubble' to get another crop the second year before giving the land a rest with a summer fallow. That third year we just cut down the weeds and preserved the moisture for the next year. 'Summer fallowing' kept the land in good heart.

135

But Khrushchev had had to have the maximum possible harvest from those Kazakh plains that year. He was a politician, he could never wait. So he had to risk the earth going dry. He knew that I appreciated this, too.

As the train rolled on, at the border between one farm and the next one we were joined by the managers who came to be presented to Mr. Khrushchev and give him their reports. Some of them came with us part of the way to point out details of the vast wheatlands. One of these managers was a woman, and she spoke to me with the help of the interpreter with what seemed a little less reserve than the men. She understood about 'summer fallowing' and I told Khrushchev, 'This woman knows the right way to farm.' And Khrushchev said, 'If you don't stop this propaganda, I'm going to put you off the train.'

When I met him at the beginning of that trip I presented Mr. Khrushchev with a rather special watch, an Accutron, the kind that runs on a little battery and a tuning fork. Khrushchev examined it quizzically. 'Is this an infernal machine you have brought to blow up Communism?' I shook my head, laughing. 'O.K.,' said Khrushchev, 'I'll take it home and let my wife try it on.'

He couldn't help it. He even played for laughs with corny jokes.

In a subsequent visit to the Kremlin, and after I had visited Mr. Kosygin, when I was asked what else I would like to do while I was in Russia, I said I would like to meet Mr. Khrushchev again and shake hands with him. I recognized that there were difficulties as he was by then out of office, but I gave them my promise that I would not publish anything that was said or done. I was then told that such a visit would be unacceptable to the Government.

Having failed to see Khrushchev, that year I went on a trip to the Island of Brioni in the Adriatic to meet

President Tito. We were holding discussions with the Yugoslav Government about going into partnership in some hotels along their coast, and it was with the Yugoslavs that I discovered that it is difficult to do business on a partnership basis with a communist country. We learned that in their hotels it was the working staffs who made the rules and decisions about the running of the hotels. 'Not with my money, they won't,' I said. We confined our proposition to block reservations.

Then there was Chairman Ceausescu of Romania—the rebel in the communist camp—who, when I said I could feel a hint of freedom in the air of his country, said he had to cope with it in other places, too, besides the air. President Zhivko Zhivkov of Bulgaria was very keen that we should do business with him, and operate in the summer resorts of the Black Sea. The Bulgarians had planned intelligently the development of their tourist business, and their hotels were acceptable to Western standards for the cheaper package tours. But none of these places has so far become really popular with the British people, who for their own good reasons seem to prefer to go to non-communist countries for their holidays.

The Bulgarians gave me a pretty high-level dinner in Sofia, and I remember noticing a little girl selling flowers in the restaurant. When, in answer to my query, I was told she wasn't working for the Government, I asked them to bring her over: I wanted to meet a Bulgarian capitalist.

Zhivkov spoke to me with great frankness and made me feel very welcome in his country, to which he has recently invited me to pay a return visit. Of course I knew he was a tough communist and his country closely follows Russian policies as they have some debts to pay the U.S.S.R.

I was fortunate to start these travels early enough to meet Pandit Nehru, an exceptional and fine man.

He said he would not allow me to own an Indian paper, although they weren't particularly happy with the Indian ownership. But later, when he agreed with the decision to start television in India and that it should be run with commercials, he told his people that they should approach me. 'Thomson will get you the best advice on this.'

That was how I later met his daughter, Mrs. Gandhi, when she became or was about to become Prime Minister. She was then a very beautiful woman but cold, preoccupied.

On other occasions we visited Mrs. Golda Meir of Israel and the oil-rich sheikhs of the Persian Gulf, the Shah of Iran himself, and the ill-fated King Faisal of Saudi Arabia, who made us understand the depth of the Arab–Jewish problem by saying that he would never recognize Israel, not even if Egypt did. More enjoyable was the visit to Beirut and to President Frangié of the Lebanon, who said he wished British business men could actually see and get to know his country. This we said could be done and some time later we took a planeload of a hundred senior men from British business with their wives to be Frangié's guests. They all confessed astonishment at the royal treatment meted out to them, a car provided for each couple for the whole of their stay and lavish hospitality, the sort of thing at which the Middle East needs no instruction from the West. At the end of our stay, there was no attempt to push business. Thomson people had already been there, and we have a majority interest in one of the two Lebanese TV stations.

Naturally one did not come away from a visit to Mr. Vorster in Pretoria so happily as from the Lebanon. My feeling when I was with him was one of relief that I didn't have to make the decisions that face him. Although one can't condone the discrimination between races that still goes on under Vorster, even in the pay for the same job, one cannot help feeling some sympathy for him in his dilemma. I reflected that I wouldn't have known what to do if I had been in his shoes, not for a start anyway.

I recall, too, having an audience with Haile Selassie before *he* was caught up in the winds of change, and noting that, although he could, as I knew, speak very good English, he used an interpreter throughout. I wondered if maybe I shouldn't have done the same thing when I was in Scotland and so have kept myself out of trouble. I asked the Emperor if I could take over the English-language paper in Addis Ababa, but found that it was owned by a Catholic institution, which ruled out a deal. I am thankful, now.

Later, when we heard of the revolution sweeping through Ethiopia, I recalled vividly the old Emperor sitting on his gilt couch and, throughout the audience, fondling a small pet dog that never left his side.

Time was running out, too, for Sir Abubakar Tafewa Balewa, the Federal Prime Minister of Nigeria, when I met him, some years before that, and I won't argue if someone says he was the finest of the African leaders. Sir Abubakar was also a very wise man, although he could not avoid (or did not want to avoid) his fate at the hands of his Army officer assassins.

We were then running two very good newspapers in Nigeria. I was very proud of them. Although we supplied the management we always had a Nigerian editor, and from time to time, one or other of the papers would criticise the Federal Prime Minister and members of his Government. Sir Abubakar eventually complained to Duncan Sandys, who was then at the Commonwealth Relations Office. The best plan, I thought, was to go out and see Sir Abubakar, knowing him to be not only Prime Minister but a great character.

All he asked was that we should remember that
Africans like his people were not accustomed to newspapers as we were in Britain; what they saw in print
they took as gospel truth, and, bearing that in mind,
would we in future try to keep our criticism on more
objective lines? But would we, he added, on no account
stop publishing our papers?

Antony (Viscount) Head, who was then High Commissioner, was very pleased with the outcome of that
conversation, and himself pleaded with us to keep the
papers going, although he knew it was costing us a lot
of money, and he reported to Harold Macmillan how
we were helping out there.

But no newspaper or wise old statesman could, by
that time, halt the march of tragic events.

Some years later—in October, 1972, to be exact—
one of these trips took us across another communist
frontier, this time into China and to a remarkable meeting with Chou En-lai. With me were Ken, my son,
Denis Hamilton and publisher George Rainbird, a
director of Thomson Publications, Frank Giles, deputy
editor of the *Sunday Times*, Louis Heren, deputy editor
of *The Times*, and David Bonavia, who was going to
Peking as correspondent of *The Times*, the first such
from a Western newspaper since the revolution.

We had several days of sight-seeing, very efficiently
organized, a few official lunches and dinners, and a
great deal of green tea which was offered us everywhere
we went. I recall that at Peking University, which
stands in lovely wooded grounds outside the city and
had then 11,000 students, the first sight to greet us was
a party of students, men and women, digging an air-raid
shelter. Mao's teaching stresses the all-round nature of
education, and enrolment to the university is from the
farm communes, the factories and the army. Most of the
students, on graduating, return to the work-bench, the

plough or the platoon, only a few being directed immediately to 'special duties'.

Likewise, teachers in colleges and higher schools,
along with members from the political cadres from all
over the vast country, go periodically for retraining at
what they call a May-7 school. We visited one of these
and talked with a group of middle-aged women teachers
sitting on their bunks in a simple dormitory. They spend
three to six months there, three and a half days each
week working on the farm alongside the peasants and
two and a half days on ideological studies. They seemed
quite happy; at least they said they were. They continued
to receive their teachers' salaries while they were being
'brought into contact with the ordinary people and
ordinary life and educated to ward off revisionism and to
promote the will to serve the whole (proletarian-run)
country.'

Driving along the country-side roads on an expedi-
tion to the Yellow River, I remember strange contrasts:
in one field a combine harvester at work, in another
nearby large numbers of peasants cutting and stacking
the wheat by hand. On many roads they had spread out
their rice crop, brown and in husk, to dry. Our cars
rolled over it, apparently without anyone minding.

Mr. Chou talked with us for three and a half hours,
with a noticeable directness and self-confidence and alert-
ness of mind which might have explained how, at 72, as
he then was, he was still in complete control of the
country and of himself, and why he had been Prime
Minister since 1949, which is a trifle longer than any of
our Western democrats can achieve.

Mr. Chou said that Eden could have established
complete diplomatic relations with China in 1954 and
could also have visited Peking, but he was undermined
by John Foster Dulles's policies. Dulles had refused to
sign the Geneva agreements on Vietnam, but had said

the U.S. would not disturb the agreements, which of course they did. Chou thanked Eden for presenting the facts in his memoirs. That was seventeen wasted years until Chairman Mao opened the door that had been closed on China.

Chou also had some scathing remarks to make about the Russians. He said they were revisionists and that Soviet imperialism was more imperialist than the old Czarist imperialism. Asked bluntly if he disliked the Russian system more than the American, he said bluntly 'Yes'.

I suggested to him that if China borrowed money to buy modern equipment they could very quickly raise the living standards of the people. If the debt was properly managed and regarded as an investment that would be mutually profitable, great projects could be successfully undertaken. But Mr. Chou shook his head and remarked that the Chinese had an old saying: 'You begin with bare hands'. They would rather raise the living standards gradually and build up the country on a basis of love and patriotism than follow India's example; India had got into debt with the U.S. for so many billion dollars that they had to take out fresh loans to pay the interest. China needed equipment and skills but would pay on delivery.

I came back again to this subject later in our talk for I always like to argue the virtues of capitalism with communist leaders. I told Mr. Chou how when I had paid for my first newspaper I borrowed more from the bank to buy my second one and from the second moved on in the same way to the third. That was how in later years we in Thomsons made our big expansion and how we were able, for instance, to take newspapers and television to the developing countries—by borrowing money from the banks. Chou smiled as he replied and his interpreter said:

'Prime Minister Chou asks is it not true then that you had a licence to print money?'

Having primed himself so thoroughly with such details of my past and using this knowledge so unexpectedly, he completely floored me.

But my newspaper colleagues were quite happy with my provocative questioning of the Prime Minister. Louis Heren, *The Times* Deputy Editor, complimented me—flattered me, indeed—by saying that if I hadn't directed my career to the commercial side of newspapers, I could, in his estimation, have become instead a successful journalist. I wonder. I don't know a Canadian proprietor who would have paid me enough.

Besides satisfying the curiosity of our news men, our trip was also concerned with the organisation of the Chinese Exhibition of archaeological finds which was to go to the Royal Academy under the sponsorship of *The Times* and the *Sunday Times* and in association with the Academy and the Great Britain/China Committee. Chou En-lai spoke warmly of this and there is no doubt the exhibition helped to improve British (and Western) relations with China, just as the Tutankhamun Exhibition, which we also sponsored, clearly improved relations with Egypt. Great newspapers like *The Times* and the *Sunday Times* have, I do believe, a responsibility to use their skills and resources in bringing to the country these great cultural treasures, which always involves an element of financial risk that they are better able to gauge and perhaps to bear than public bodies are.

One other world leader I got to know rather well was President Nixon. I had entertained him in London after his defeat by Kennedy and his subsequent failure to become Governor of California, and he appeared to appreciate being fêted when his position was at its then lowest ebb. Later, when he was President he invited me to dinner at the White House when the Prince of Wales and Princess Anne were there.

Another President with whom I had an agreeable time was Gamal Abdel Nasser. I recall that when I was with him I asked him if he would like me to take over his country's English-language newspaper, the *Egyptian Gazette*, which I knew was losing money fast. He said he would, 'but you will have to pay me for it.'

'You're not an Arab, you're a Jew,' I told him. This seemed to tickle him greatly. But even if he was pleased to laugh at my little joke, he was still not going to get me to pay for his *Gazette*.

Of course, I got to know our own political leaders better than any of these foreign potentates. Of the two great protagonists, Harold Wilson and Ted Heath, I must say that I took more readily to Mr. Wilson though I don't like his politics. He is a very likeable man and easier to get to know. He told me many things in confidence and he never equivocated with me. In public he has to defend the Party's policies and sometimes kow-tow to the wishes of the unions, but I am convinced that, if he had his own way at all times, many of his policies would be different.

Ted Heath is of a different stamp, but a man of great courage and integrity. We did get on good terms but it took longer. I remember being at Chequers when the Gulf sheikhs were there. You know how these luncheons drag on. That day I was extremely anxious to get to our new plant at Hemel Hempstead before it closed for the day. I asked the P.M. if he would excuse me, saying that I wouldn't dream of dragging myself away except that it was costing me money to stay. Ted immediately asked the company, 'What do you think of this Canadian? I invite him to lunch and he tells me that it is costing him money!'

I was very happy to support Mr. Heath in his campaign to take Britain into the Common Market. I made a series of speeches to various gatherings at home and abroad, mostly after-lunch or after-dinner efforts but usually in influential company; this was something in which I very sincerely believed. I feel deeply that Britain would have a difficult future without the support of the bigger group.

I found it wasn't easy to get to know Harold Macmillan, either, but after I had stayed with him, though we may not have been on the same intellectual level, we became very close friends. I was always entranced by his brilliant talk and his flow of ideas, and I have been more proud of his friendship than of almost anything else that has happened to me since coming to stay in Britain.

What these British statesmen appreciated about me, I dare say, besides my frankness and lack of pretension, was that I had no axe to grind, no personal campaign to run in my papers as other proprietors sometimes had, no ambition to be a king-maker. They could take me as they found me, and they could always evaluate my advice as being at least sincere.

9

THE INNOVATORS

MEANWHILE WE were beginning to introduce other, and perhaps more consequential,
innovations. In one or two of our acquisitions at
this time I took a particular pride.

Our theme in diversifying the business was to take
into other fields of communication such skills and experience as we had been building up in the running of our
newspapers, and later in Thomson Publications. A very
different kind of communication had been practised by
Monty Hyams in his small firm, Derwent Publications,
when we took a 51 per cent interest in it. It circulated information about patents and also sent to its clients abstracts
from technical and learned scientific journals, its clients
being science-based manufacturing companies in the U.K.
and overseas. When Derwent joined us it was developed
rapidly until it was employing over three hundred
scientists, fifty of them on the staff, and it provides an
indispensable service to leading industrial organisations
throughout the world and principally in the United States,
Japan and West Germany. It has introduced the first
major and comprehensive Central Patents Index. This
supplies industry for the first time with the means of
making full use quickly and economically of all the technological innovations and developments wherever in the
world they may first appear; and it alerts subscribers to

146

new patents and acts as a source of information for research and development projects. The spread of this information is so important to the modern world that in this branch of our activities our communications take the form not only of books and magazines but of magnetic tapes and punched cards and micro-film.

A curious parallel to this enterprise took place about the same time, this one being an activity of Thomson International, which formed the Kraus-Thomson Company. Hans Kraus was known then as the most important rare book dealer. But he, with his colleague, Fred Altman, had also developed a method of reprinting rare books for universities and scholastic institutions. We liked what he was doing and joined him in a company to expand the whole business of rare books and scholastic material of great antique importance. Hans had built up access to all this material, in its original form, through his purchase of rare books and his discovery of where they could be found. When the demand for any of that antique material went beyond the possibility of supply by buying and selling, it was time to reprint a small edition, and this decision was always taken when the last available copy of the book or manuscript was in his hands. So we not only had the materials but the best kind of market indicator to tell us when we must produce and sell. Hans Kraus had perfected the reprint production, and his ability to supply a limited number of these old books in reprint form was of immense importance to universities everywhere.

Kraus-Thomson operates from Lichtenstein, and if you think it could be one of these convenient one-roomed office corporations which inhabit that place, you are far from the truth. We have, in fact, a very big plant there and an inventory of some five million books. We have another large plant in New York State, and there, too, a vast amount of books ready to hand. The company is undoubtedly the main reservoir in the world of this

147

scholarly material, and I am proud to have my name and my team associated with it. This was another way to use our profits from TV and the newspapers, and a development of a kind that gave us a lot of satisfaction.

The years 1961 to 1971 certainly gave us a very exciting decade. We didn't need to go beyond the bank to get ample credit at 6 per cent and it was upon that, substantially, that the massive expansion of the Organisation was built; on that and on a team ready to dig in and develop anywhere. In the autumn of 1964 a two-day meeting at Liphook, at Jim Coltart's house, of the executive board produced very good reasons for expanding not only faster but farther than up to then we had done.

There were good reasons why we couldn't count on a continuation of our profits, nor was it likely that we could forge ahead with expansion in the newspaper field. Scottish Television was more than ever vulnerable to political intervention because of a genuine feeling in the country that for one company to control the leading newspaper as well as the television station was not in the public interest. There had, too, been criticism of STV, especially from Scots of nationalist views, who complained that the programme was not Scottish enough. This criticism might have been ill-informed, but it could be used against us when the contract came up for renewal.

We were then becoming convinced—and we were proved right very soon—that in the years immediately ahead it would not be so practicable to continue expanding by acquiring from time to time the ownership of other British newspapers. This kind of acquisition was likely to be controlled in future. There was a growing feeling against the powers of the media being available for purchase without any restraint. The development of Thomson Publications into the magazine, periodical and book worlds had gone ahead with great success, and had been successfully diversified into service and information retrieval business. But now we must also seek new pastures for this division, as well as for the available forces and funds of the newspaper company. Gordon Brunton was put in charge of this operation, with a small group of helpers freed from other commitments.

The idea of Yellow Pages had been in train for some time. This was very much a personal idea. Why, I kept on asking, why is it that in the States and Canada and in other developed countries a sophisticated telephone directory functioned with a classified section giving all the trades and professions and shops and so on under their separate headings, and why wasn't there such a thing in Britain? It would not only be a sell-out from the advertising angle, for all the categories would rush to pay for having their businesses included, but it would be a public service that had long been needed, and you may have noticed throughout my career a great liking for making a profit out of doing a public service. But how else, in Britain, if you didn't know his name, did you call a plumber in an emergency?

We discovered that the company who had the contract for finding advertising for the British phone books had had that contract for twenty-odd years, that no one had suggested that there should be any changes, and that the contract came up for tender in about a year's time. We put a team to study the performance and methods of the directories in other countries, and when we saw how profitably and well it could be done, we tendered for the contract and, winning it without trouble, then sold the Post Office the idea of a classified directory for every area of the country, which was a lot of advertising.

Yet this was what even I would call a traumatic experience for all of us. Even in a big modern organisation like ours, where every second man seems to be carrying a pocket computer or a slide-rule, people can get their sums wrong. We had undoubtedly got the scheme right in concept and in organisation; but we had, alas, been given the wrong figures in the projections of the operation. The estimate of the speed at which we could collect the insertions and publish the directories in all the areas had, somewhere along the line, got snarled up. We were hopelessly wrong in these projections. We were years out. You can figure what that meant: paying wages, running a business, knowing that there could be no profit for years. But we were stuck with the job to do and the losses to be borne.

The shock waves receded. If the principle is right and if your purse is long enough, you get over the difficulties. It took between seven and eight years to make Yellow Pages a part of the vocabulary. But we made it, and it was an important development for the country and for the Post Office, and doubly so for the Thomson Organisation. We learned how to keep our nerve and carry on when something was going seriously wrong, and we battled on until we could begin to bring in the harvest.

Meanwhile Gordon was searching for the entirely new pastures that would suit us. Away from the communications business altogether, he set himself to find:

(a) a growth industry;
(b) a business not requiring deep technical know-how;
(c) an operation with a cash flow that worked on a different cycle from that of newspapers;
(d) an industry that would employ the skills we had built up, and particularly that let us do what we were best at—selling to consumers in the marketplace; in other words, a market-orientated company.

For all these reasons, having examined closely some forty to fifty companies and their operations, he plumped for the travel business.

The package holiday industry had been started by Vladimir Raitz with Horizon Holidays Ltd. It seemed ripe in 1965 for a dramatic take-off. What Raitz had discovered and Captain Teddy Langton had further developed was that, if you made a business of it and organised everything well in advance, if you chartered aircraft, booking thousands of seats, and reserved blocks of bedrooms, if not entire hotels, and if you put clever advertisements in the way of people who had never thought of going abroad, you could sell them a fortnight on the Mediterranean, including aircraft, all meals and hotel, for less than the cost of the scheduled air-fare to that particular spot. With the spending power of the new technological age working people, wouldn't millions go for that?

Gordon based his faith on the expansion that would come from the great mysteries of the British climate and that enormously increasing spending power of the ordinary people. In cost terms, they could have a holiday in the Mediterranean sun in a comparatively high quality hotel for less than they would be asked to pay to sit and watch the rain from a Blackpool boarding-house. Moreover, since a deposit was payable on every booking, the cash would begin to flow in the winter and the spring, just when newspapers were habitually getting in little money, and by the time we had to pay for the hotels the newspaper income would be rising again to meet the demands.

We had an added advantage in being able to communicate through our newspapers and magazines to millions of prospective clients; in other words we could make our sales of inclusive holiday tours in the advertisement columns of our own newspapers, and that very likely at a time—at the beginning of the year—when these columns were not carrying their full load. This would be cross-fertilization between one area and another of the Organisation's activities, which was good economic sense.

The idea was to take over Sky Tours from Captain

Langton and also Riviera Holidays, his main rival, as well as a small airline, Britannia Airways, owned by Teddy Langton and J. E. D. Williams.

The project was presented to us by Gordon Brunton in the board-room of Elm House (that was a new office block which we had built behind the old Kemsley House). He had called the accountants to examine the balance sheets and the projections and to give their views of the proposal. We had found an opening in the travel business fairly early in its developing story; this can be judged by the fact that Sky Tours had not yet shown a profit (which was not to say that it wasn't doing well). Nor, of course, were there any assets, apart from three or four Britannia aircraft. Only goodwill and shrewd faith.

I don't think I have ever heard a less favourable report than what the accountants gave that day. In our three hours' discussion a great deal was also said about what could go wrong with Gordon's scheme. I didn't say anything until all this had been aired and then I said I wanted to go ahead with Gordon's proposal. 'I think he may be right,' I said.

Our marketing director raised some doubts about including an airline in the scheme. He had the idea that ordinary working people would not go for aircraft travel. They might stick stubbornly to rail travel. Or the aircraft itself might soon give place to helicopters. 'Or camels,' someone said, and a low Scots voice (Jim Coltart's) added: 'We might do well in the camel trade,' This, though said in a joke, was exactly the spirit I favoured, and the project was adopted. We went into the travel business.

We did very well in our first couple of years as inclusive tour operators. But it was a business that, as it expanded, certainly needed strong nerves. It became the most brutally competitive industry that I have ever known. Only now with the death of Clarksons and

Horizon is it beginning to moderate and operators are no longer ready to sell at cut-throat prices and to accept far too small a return for their money and trouble.

Both Thomson Directories Ltd (Yellow Pages) and Thomson Holidays began in 1965, and in that same year, thirty-one years after I had bought my first newspaper in northern Ontario for 600 dollars down, we went out on a limb to start a new newspaper, and not only the first to be started in Britain for many years but the first in the world to be produced on web-offset assisted by computer.

Thirty-one years ago in Timmins, northern Ontario, I had bought a weekly newspaper and within a few months turned it into a daily. A slight shift in that procedure was adopted in Reading, England: here I bought a weekly with the plan already made to turn it into an evening paper. The resemblance with Timmins falls short in other directions, too. For the advance in technology in those thirty-one years was simply staggering.

Nobody had attempted to launch a new evening paper in Britain since Rothermere had a go at establishing a string of *Evening Worlds* in provincial cities and he found it such a battle then that, in the end, he was apparently obliged to be satisfied with only one, in Bristol. Nobody had even attempted a serious study of the possibilities since before the war. But I had a feeling that this was a wasteful oversight.

I had a hunch that there were areas in Britain which had never been appraised as possible centres for newspapers and which might be just the place for them in the greatly changed world I was now contemplating. No one in England had begun to think of running an evening paper with a small circulation and small costs as we do in America. We therefore set our team of experts to work, and in due course they came up with certain places they had singled out as likely to provide an economic basis for an evening paper.

We then tackled the formidable problem of reducing the cost of producing such a newspaper; we had a hope of successful production in three or four places if we could get the formula right: small circulation, no competition, low costs. We believed we had a technological break-through and in a place like Reading, when we would be creating printing jobs that hadn't existed before, we believed we could bargain with the unions. We could get their agreement, for the first time in Britain, to our introduction of full-scale automation in the newspaper business.

That agreement was finally achieved, and we laid down a plant that was the first of its kind in the world, with computer-assisted photo-composition, and web-offset printing. By this combination we could and did produce a better-looking newspaper, with high quality typesetting and pictures, and we could produce it with much less labour than by the traditional ways. We finally convinced the unions that if we couldn't produce a paper like that then we wouldn't be able to have a paper at all.

The Reading *Evening Post* became an established success, and already, in 1965, we were planning how we could carry out the idea I had of ringing London with a chain of evening papers. These papers would be essentially local in character, unlike the London evenings; they would be viable because they would generate a great deal of purely local advertising, a source of newspaper support still comparatively little exploited in the U.K., and they would compete with the London evening papers because they would give the local news and the local advertising and they would print the London and national news hours after the suburban editions of the *Evening Standard* and the *Evening News* had been bundled on to the vans, for delivery to these distant commuter towns.

After studying the research we had done, it seemed to

me there was an ideal place to begin this development—
in the area around the towns of Luton and Watford. In
the neighbourhoods of these two towns, which we could
take as central points, were other satellite towns like
Welwyn, Stevenage and St. Albans. In these, business as
well as population was expanding. It seemed that we
could produce two papers, one for the Luton area and the
other for Watford, at one production centre and there
was a good spot for that in the new town of Hemel
Hempstead, where we very soon found an empty
building. In this we installed two web-offset presses and
one computer to assist the photo-setting of both papers,
and we thought we were all fixed. While staff were being
engaged, we began to meet separately the two union
general secretaries, John Bonfield of the National
Graphical Association (NGA) and Richard Briginshaw of
the National Society of Operative Printers and Assistants
(NATSOPA). With them we had to come to an agreement about staffing the machines realistically and not
like those presses in London where over-manning is still
rife. In this way we ran head-on into the perpetual
problem of the newspaper industry in Britain, the problem that threatens today more than ever to extinguish
some fine papers and deprive thousands of skilled men of
their livelihood.

At 81 I think I am old enough to have got over most of
the bias and the bitterness I once had in this matter. I
may be old enough even to be believed, as few who take
part in these industrial wrangles can always hope to be.
So I think I should tell the story of this classic dispute, as
it were from the inside and in some detail. Suddenly and
unexpectedly it became for us a big gamble—£2,500,000
was at stake—and we came very near to losing it.

At our first meeting, Mr. Bonfield of NGA agreed
to a number of men on the machines which I thought very
reasonable. Mr. (now Lord) Briginshaw said he would

co-operate, too; he was just as anxious to see new papers started and new jobs created for his members. Certainly he would agree to realistic staffing of the presses, always provided, of course, that his members had parity with the NGA minders.

This was the tip of the iceberg showing and we should have known what to expect next. The NGA is by tradition the craft union, embracing the machine-minders, linotype operators, readers, stereotypers, compositors and press telegraphists, whereas NATSOPA takes in all sorts and conditions, from press-workers and packers to wire-room messengers, from cleaners to clerks and cashiers. Between the two unions there has never been a shortage of antagonism. In the quarrelsome past there may have been some poaching. Mr. Bonfield, at our next meeting, said flatly No, his men would be in charge of the presses and would have full responsibility. They would not accept equal status with NATSOPA, or any notion of sharing the tasks and letting NATSOPA handle on occasion the prime jobs. To this Mr. Briginshaw retorted that his men were not second-class citizens. Equal status was something they had been fighting for for a long time. 'However,' he said, 'if the traditional relationship is to be maintained, there is no problem: we will just staff up the presses at Hemel Hempstead with the traditional Fleet Street numbers.' In other words, there would be no flexibility of job between the two unions, and NATSOPA now wanted for each machine, brake hands, fly-hands, oilers, broom hands and all the other toilers of the Fleet Street night, most of whose duties are so specialized and so limited that their lives must become very wearisome indeed.

I was not going to agree to such a suicidal arrangement. It had wrecked old and well-established papers. It would completely destroy our chances at Hemel in the fight with the London evenings we knew we would have to face. In the meantime recruiting had gone ahead and, including journalists, who had given up jobs in different parts of the country because they saw new career possibilities at Hemel, about two hundred people were already on the books. In view of the complete impasse between the two unions the prospects for these two hundred were grim. And Christmas (1966) was not far off.

Feeling very sore about this, I went off to Canada for my usual family Christmas, and I remember telling an *Evening Standard* reporter at the airport that I was abandoning my plans for new evening papers in view of union intractability. In Hemel, they had begun sending people home and paying them compensation for loss of their jobs and helping a few to find work elsewhere.

But Eric Cheadle, the Thomson Organisation deputy managing director, who had handled the negotiations, contrived to continue meeting Mr. Bonfield and Mr. Briginshaw informally, looking for a little bit of give here and there that might produce some compromise in the stiff problem of the differentials. And in the meantime the TUC were brought, not altogether eagerly, into the picture. Some of the disappointed Hemel employees marched on Congress House with banners protesting against losing their jobs through the quarrel of the two unions. George Woodcock was General Secretary at the time and Victor Feather his assistant. With the latter Eric Cheadle had, through the years, developed a close and valuable friendship, and he now got in touch with him and pointed out that the same two unions were working amicably enough together on the web-offset printing of the Northern Ireland edition of the *Daily Mirror* at Belfast, where it had been transferred from Manchester not long before. He was later told by Vic Feather that a deputation from the special committee of the TUC, which dealt with demarcation disputes between unions, was going to Belfast to see how the two unions' men were working together there. Mr. Bonfield and Mr. Briginshaw were both on this deputation and in the plane on the way back the former was called into conclave with Mr. Woodcock, Mr. Feather and Mr. (now Lord) Cooper, who were bemoaning the sorry reflection that was being cast on trade unionism, when a chance to find more prosperous employment for more people in an important industry was being lost through an inter-union disagreement. Mr. Bonfield showed a new willingness to move in certain directions, provided, he said, Dick Briginshaw would make some concessions, which he didn't think the other man would.

As it happened, Eric Cheadle went to the Christmas party given at NATSOPA headquarters and getting Mr. Briginshaw into a corner eventually persuaded him to promise that he would not object to the minders (NGA) being in charge of the presses at Hemel so long as it was understood that his NATSOPA men would have the opportunity of promotion to being minders in certain circumstances.

Shortly afterwards, Vic Feather phoned Eric to ask if he would accept some kind of arrangement that would apply only to Hemel Hempstead and would not set up a precedent for the staffing of presses elsewhere in the future. Eric said he would agree to anything that would save the situation at Hemel, but he didn't think this move was likely to succeed. About one o'clock that day, however, someone brought him a P.A. snap (news-flash) from the wire-room. It stated that a solution had been found to the Hemel Hempstead problem. The news had been given by Vic Feather.

So the project was finally got off the ground, with fairly reasonable manning, though not as economical as we had originally expected, and not without considerable losses due to the delay in starting, which had been further extended by having to wait for a suitable period of the year for launching the new papers.

That, of course, was just the beginning of another struggle. We had a tough fight with the two London papers, in an area they had dominated so long, to find a viable circulation for the new papers. Free copies of the *Standard* and the *News* were at different times and frequencies dropped on the doorsteps of the Luton and Watford lieges while our fledgling papers were cried round the streets of these and other towns. The *Standard* and the *News* swamped the market so that many people didn't bother to buy any evening paper. But we had the enormous advantage of the new techniques, better printing, later news and a truly local service. The winning advantage, which we had counted on from the distant origins of this project, was in local announcements and advertisements, the births, marriages and deaths, which give even commuters a sense of community and sometimes opportunities they cannot afford to ignore. We went on for long enough pouring good money down the drain, publishing and selling at enormous loss, but we never really thought that we would lose the fight.

After that, and after the refusal of the unions to accord us any hope of future amicable arrangements between themselves, the idea of a chain of papers like these three we had started began to lose the impetus it once had had. Of this I have something to say in a later chapter.

Newspaper people in Britain hadn't yet come to realize that a newspaper's primary hope of success was its ability to sell advertising space, and that this as much as the provision of a news service was the business of newspaper companies, a highly complex business requiring a whole range of skills and new techniques, and there was no call to go weeping about 'lack of support' and about newspapers going to the wall if these skills and techniques were not being used.

I still can't get over the antipathy I find in Britain to the art and skill of salesmanship. Napoleon used to call the English a nation of shop-keepers, but that must have altered a long time ago. Although nowadays there are some firms which are noticeable exceptions, the general run of British businessmen still instinctively look down on hard selling. The almost universal attitude is 'I make good stuff and the public don't need to be told.' Every firm has something to sell, even if it is only their reputation, and if it doesn't sell hard what it has got to offer, it is still living at the turn of the century, and it certainly can't count on survival far less success just because its chairman is a member of the right club and its sales director, so called, wears the right tie. No modern business can stay with success unless it goes on working to its full potential and that demands a strong sales force. Yet when our regional offices learned that George Pappas was going to visit them to fix up a team of tele-ad girls and train them how to do their work, some of them, believe it or not, asked to be passed by, would we send Pappas elsewhere, taking the line that these American methods would never work in Wigan or wherever, and look at the harm they would have to undo.

We found George Pappas working in the States, an advertising consultant teaching sales girls in a city newspaper office how to sell by telephone. We suspected that there was so much to teach and to expand in that business that we asked him if he would come over and spend a year or two with us. Our suspicion was right: George brought a real revolution into the British newspaper industry. What he taught may ultimately have saved *The Times*; it certainly saved several other papers throughout the country from going down.

He employed every possible technique of persuasion on the telephone and went right through every kind of directory and list to find people who might want to advertise. He hired big staffs to do this, in most offices as many as fifty, mostly young girls, not because they were cheaper, though perhaps they were, but because they could learn better how to carry out his ideas. George taught them not only what to say but how to say it, to learn all over again how to speak, in fact. Many of them went home in tears, but those who made the grade vied with their colleagues to win extra money for results.

Variations of the telephone sale were practised hard. If twenty people had advertised the week before, they were all worth phoning, for two might agree to repeat. Subtly appealing additions were suggested when anyone dictated an advertisement. Three- or four-line small ads. of the fifties became the four inches double column semi-display ad. of the sixties. With boom time in British industry Pappas and Co. tackled the 'appointments' advertisement that offered jobs ranging from managing director to personal assistant. In Aberdeen, Newcastle, Wales and London, wherever we operated, the sales talk convinced the companies who were looking for highly paid staff that they had their own prestige to consider every time they advertised, apart altogether from attracting the right kind of smart man. Few of these firms considered in the years that followed that where once a discreet four-line notice had been sufficient and proper, it would be a waste of money paying four or five hundred pounds for a prestigious display of their requirements and importance.

This was how the great expansion in the size of newspapers was financed. And it was not by chance that other newspapers, in seeking advertising assistants, frequently included the words, 'must be Thomson trained'. Even today, long after George Pappas has gone back to the States, the training of telephone sales girls goes on in the Thomson Organisation offices every hour of the working day.

The sensational rise of the classified section in our papers may seem a small matter to have taken up so much of my attention. The Pappas revolution did, as I have said, save several newspapers from going to the wall, I am convinced, and it enabled other, successful papers like the *Sunday Times* so substantially to increase their size and their revenue—ten or twelve pages of appointments every week were not unusual—that they were able to shoulder the penal cost of their labour troubles.

Of course, in this period of thrusting growth, some mistakes were inevitable. Gordon Brunton has reminded me about the Mussolini diaries, for the odd reason that this illustrates the confidence he and other directors had in me. They knew how I would react.

It was also a good story. The approach came to Denis Hamilton who talked to Gordon about the book rights as well as the serial. A part of the manuscript was produced. Thirty diaries apparently existed, one kept each year of his career as Il Duce by Benito Mussolini. They had all been found in a suitcase among his possessions when he and his mistress, Clara Petacci, were captured and later shot by partisans near Milan while the German army scrambled out of Italy.

Gordon had the handwriting examined by a graphologist. He had the manuscript paper tested and the ink analysed and dated chemically. Handwriting, ink and paper all fitted. So did the things written, when translated and read by an eminent historian, correspond with what Mussolini had been in fact doing at the time in question and what he would quite likely have said, as gauged by people who had made a study of his character and his career. It was the publishing find of the post-war epoch!

The diaries appeared to be full of historically important material and at the same time of fascinating and very exciting and readable accounts of life in the Palazzo Venezia, a first-hand account by the dictator himself. No wonder my people were excited. Obviously if we got those diaries they could be resold all over the world, the serialization might have to be published in several sections at intervals, the books in more than one volume.

The deal was negotiated. The first payment—a six-figure sum—was made. At this point, one other thing they might have done occurred to the Thomson executives concerned. They were not even clear about what they were looking for. But someone went into a newspaper office in Milan to go through the Mussolini cuttings . . .

And there it was. The story of how twenty years before, just after the war, two forgers had produced the Mussolini diaries. Not our manuscript. A previous one. It had also been proved then that no such manuscript had been found with Mussolini, or later in his archives.

I was in Gordon's room, asking 'What news?', when he told me. It was a substantial sum that had flown with the confidence men. Gordon recalls that I then asked: 'How much would we have made if the diaries had turned out to be genuine?'

He told me—it would have been the publishing *coup* of the century.

'Well,' I said, 'it was worth taking the chance.'

I then asked him if he would have someone look into my driver being paid overtime for taking me home in the evening. Was that necessary and right?

Gordon Brunton introduced something soon afterwards that was a very successful publishing innovation. This was the selling of magazines prepared specially for supermarkets and sold exclusively in these stores. Thomson Publications had for some time been looking for the opportunity to enter the vast women's magazine market without committing commercial suicide. As I have explained, Cecil King had spent a great deal of money combining Odhams magazines with Fleetway's in order to stop the murderous competition. Any publisher who fancied making a debut in those perfumed pastures required his head examined. Yet, if the bulk of Thomson Publications' revenue came from advertising, they naturally hated being excluded from probably the best advertising market of all.

Gordon Brunton had observed in America in the supermarkets that a glossy colour magazine was prominently offered for sale at the check point. He saw how the women, as they were about to go through the pay channel with their baskets, were obliged to wait in a small queue just where the magazine rack was and how many of them took up a copy and put it into their baskets with their groceries. On his return to Britain he looked into this business and found that Geoffrey Perry had developed this publishing concept in connection with the Sainsbury chain of shops. Geoffrey Perry and his colleagues sold their business to Thomson Publications and took on the responsibility for developing this publishing concept across the whole supermarket business in the United Kingdom. We formed a partnership with Cowles Communications Inc., the American publishers, to produce *Family Circle* on this side of the Atlantic and made an arrangement with several supermarket chains to supply them with the magazine and its specially designed selling-point rack.

It was a great success. *Family Circle*, which later became a wholly English production, though it had to be printed on the Continent, and entirely owned by us, is now the top-selling women's monthly in the country. A companion magazine, started later, called *Living* and sold in supermarkets in the same way, is now third in the country.

This particular development in the women's magazine market with *Family Circle* and with *Living* was no mean achievement and we had every reason to be proud of it.

10

TAKING CARE OF *THE TIMES*

FROM THE start of our sojourn in London it was natural that Jim Coltart and I should often talk about having a daily paper to run in conjunction with the *Sunday Times*. No Sunday newspaper could be run with the maximum success except in such an association with a daily, which would share the costs of an office and of the massive investment in machinery, remembering that the same amount of machinery is needed for a once-a-week production as for an every-day sale. When we were given notice and had to leave Fleet Street and install our own plant in Gray's Inn Road simply to print one paper a week, we knew that we could not stay for ever with that unbalanced equation. Apart from the uneconomic usage of all that plant, it is suicidal on other accounts for a Sunday paper to be run on its own. Working in tandem with a daily, the Sunday paper can share a great many services and staff.

At this time I put out feelers to Lord Rothermere about his *Daily Mail*, which looked as if it might need a new hand on its controls, and it was said that every time Rothermere felt a flutter in his heart, which had been giving him some trouble, he would receive a call on the telephone from me, asking if he did not want to rid himself of the burden of his paper. I assure you there wasn't a glimmer of truth in that story. It was true that sometimes Rothermere seemed ready to consider entering into negotiations with me, but at other times he would laugh at the idea.

Then when we learned that Lord Cadbury was thinking of divesting himself of the *Star*, we let him know that we were very interested. It was a great shock to Fleet Street and to us when it was announced that he had sold the paper to Associated News to be incorporated with their big-circulation *Evening News*, and that London was to be reduced to two evening papers, and many journalists and newspaper workers lost their jobs. The country has had many benefactions from the Cadbury family, but this was obviously a time for retrenchment, and it was no doubt the most advantageous deal to sell to the adjacent *News*, which needed the extra printing capacity while we certainly didn't.

But of all the daily papers in London, clearly *The Times*, with its title, its not dissimilar approach, its supreme reputation, and the tremendous boost it would give to our reputation—and our ego—would be the best for us to link with.

I talked it over with Jim Coltart and Denis Hamilton, and we agreed that, when I felt that it could be done casually, I should approach Lord Astor in the South of France, where he was by then domiciled because of the danger of death duties working havoc in his estate, and where I still had my villa. In 1963 I made a tentative approach, saying that I didn't believe *The Times* would be making much profit these days and that it might be of benefit to both of us if we could form some sort of association. I made no suggestion of buying or taking over; a loose form of association might include the sharing of machinery and other services that would benefit us both. Even this innocuous approach seemed to raise Lord Astor's hackles; he was reluctant to face the realities of his own position; or he didn't like my style. For whatever

Distinguished luncheon guests at Thomson House, November 1965: The Archbishop of Canterbury, Mr Richard Nixon, Mr Henry Grunfeld of S. G. Warburg (inventor of the reverse take-over bid that secured Kemsley Newspapers for Thomson's) and Mr J. M. Coltart, Deputy Chairman of Thomson's.

October, 1973: unveiling a plaque on Greenwood House, Salisbury Court, Fleet Street, where the first *Sunday Times* was edited, with Lord Thomson are (left to right) Mr C. D. Hamilton, Chairman of Times Newspapers, Mr Godfrey Smith and Mr J. W. Lambert of the *Sunday Times*, and Lord Snowdon

London, October 1963: congratulations to Mary Quant after the Duchess of Buccleuch had presented her with the *Sunday Times* International Design Award

As Colonel-in-chief of Toronto Scottish Regiment, with Queen Elizabeth the Queen Mother during her Canadian Tour, June 1962

Greeting Princess Margaret at the Ritz, April 1963, when H.R.H. presented the Ambassador Awards for Achievement

Illustrated London News 125th anniversary: Mr Gordon Brunton, Thomson Organization Managing Director, with Lord Thomson, greets the Prime Minister, May 1967

Foyle's luncheon, May 1969: Lord Thomson welcomed by Mr Hugh Cudlipp, then Chairman of International Publishing Corporation, and Mr Cecil King, the former Chairman of I.P.C.

reason he showed no eagerness even to consider what I might be suggesting.

If he hadn't, other people had been conscious for years of the declining fortunes of *The Times*. To most people in the newspaper business it seemed that the great paper, unless something drastic was done, was heading for serious trouble. An alliance with the *Sunday Times* was the best help they could get. We didn't push it, however; if we were too thrusting, we felt sure we would be inviting a blunt refusal.

I did mention the idea, very vaguely, to Gavin Astor, Lord Astor's son and heir, but he didn't seem to think I was serious. At this period the Astors didn't appear to realize that *The Times* needed such an alliance for its own survival; of course they knew *The Times* wasn't making money, but that had happened before, and it would surely recover again. But Francis Matthew and Stanley Morison, whom I met at this time, and who both had a great deal to do with the running of *The Times*, were perceptibly concerned about the paper. They were also inclined to believe that a link with us was the best hope. Neither of them, however, felt that he could mention it to Lord Astor; they were plainly afraid to broach such a matter with him.

In 1965 Denis Hamilton had three or four meetings with Gavin Astor, and in the course of friendly discussions tried to convince him that time was running out for *The Times*. Their circulation had been on a plateau for a long time, and they did not seem to realize that this was not a good sign. Quality paper circulation had been rising generally. As the quality market expanded and *The Times* stood still, conversely *The Times* became a dearer advertising medium, for their advertising rate per reader became higher in comparison with the other quality papers, and this was something that was observed without any emotion by advertising agents. What *The*

Times needed, Denis Hamilton suggested to Gavin Astor, was a transfusion of technical, marketing and managerial know-how. I knew that Cecil King was giving them similar advice, but whether, at this point, it had filtered through to Lord Astor was another matter.

Gavin Astor then arranged for Denis to go to lunch and to have Sir William Haley and George Pope join them. Sir William was chief executive as well as editor of *The Times*, Francis Matthew having died in early 1965. George, now Sir George, Pope was general manager. Gavin wanted them to hear what Denis had to say and to question him on it. Denis told them that what *The Times* urgently needed was more pages; anyone in Fleet Street who could see the frequent 36-page *Daily Telegraph* and the regular 16-page *Times* would have told them the same thing. He knew, of course, that it was the shortage of advertising that limited the size of *The Times*, but Astor and Haley didn't think they could go out to attract more advertising. Denis recounted how he had started the Business News section of the *Sunday Times* two years previously for this reason and how the new section had had to be increased on some Sundays to 24 pages, with a resultant enlargement of editorial space throughout the whole paper. This was the sort of thing *The Times* would have to plan for the paper, for their foreign reporting and cultural coverage were both lacking consistent space. The following day he received a note from Printing House Square, saying they had been glad of his advice but that they preferred to 'go it alone'.

In occasional meetings with Kenneth Keith, who was financial adviser to *The Times*, I mentioned the idea of some form of association between us and always asked him if any progress had been made towards this, but he never gave me any hope that it would come to anything. *The Times* then made its big drive, putting news on the front page, glory be, with a great deal of publicity about the 'top people', and we learned that they secured a 10 per cent increase in circulation. This, however, only made the rates they had been charging for advertising less expensive and did not enable them to increase their revenue. About two months later, in August 1966, Denis kept a long-standing engagement to lunch with Kenneth Keith and he was astonished to be asked, the moment they met, whether they could devote their conversation to discussing a possible partnership with the *Sunday Times.*

In those few weeks, after seeing what their expensive 'push' had done for them, *The Times* people had completely changed their attitudes and their opinions. The fact was that they were losing nearly sixpence on every copy they sold, and with an increased circulation but no increase in advertising revenue, the loss was all the greater, about £225,000 a year in fact.

Sir William Haley saw that to save themselves they needed more than a few changes in the paper; they needed an injection of capital, something in the region of £4m. he reckoned at that time. Cecil King, I believe, had told them that we were the only people who could save them. This wat a funny quirk of fate, for he, of course, was the man who had in effect taken Odhams from us. His was the voice, too, to which I was told *The Times* people paid most attention.

We had thought a lot about a possible merger. It was obvious that there were considerable difficulties to overcome. *The Times* was not just another newspaper; it was a bastion of empire and a pillar of the establishment, and so on. Accepting all this, I had put forward an idea of a kind of constitutional device that might get round the Astors' extreme reluctance to link their business with anyone else's. I suggested that we could form a new company into which we would put the highly successful *Sunday Times* and they would put *The Times.*

The *Sunday Times*'s annual profit had climbed to £1,200,000, and with that kind of revenue the new company would obviously be able to provide a strong crutch for *The Times* until, after a period in which it was able to spend much more on itself, *The Times* would once again become able to support itself. Thomsons and the Astors would each appoint four members to the board of the new company but, on top of that, they would each appoint two 'national' directors, public men who would be activated only by the desire to see *The Times* continue. These four 'national' directors would provide, in constitutional terms, a 'blocking third', which would ensure that neither Thomsons nor Astors would get their own way unless they could win the votes of the 'national' directors, and carry them with them in any decision.

It was an elaboration of this idea that Denis Hamilton discussed that day with Kenneth Keith as a possible basis for a merger. Kenneth Keith was inclined to think that the constitutional device would get over the main obstacle. The main obstacle was undoubtedly me. I don't think Lord Astor could stomach the idea of giving some control of his paper to a rough-neck Canadian. He would never have considered the merger if it hadn't been that Denis Hamilton was there, and he was a man they had all learned greatly to respect.

Having begun negotiations on these lines, Denis then tracked me down in the wilds of northern Ontario where I was on holiday; it took him two days to get a message to me, and that brought me running to the nearest telephone. I learned all that had been said and unhesitatingly authorized Denis to carry on until a final financial settlement had to be decided. I was back in London by the beginning of September to arrange the concluding details.

It was perhaps the oddest deal I had ever made. For I was negotiating an amalgamation of *The Times* and the

Sunday Times under a new company, and at the same time I was agreeing to rule myself out of the new company. I was agreeing to give up the income of the *Sunday Times* and in return I wasn't even to have a say in the running of *The Times*. This was to be the new set-up of Times Newspapers Ltd.:

Gavin Astor would be life president and Sir William Haley chairman, but the latter appointment would only be for two years, which was all Sir William wanted, and then my son, Kenneth, would take over from him. Denis Hamilton would be editor-in-chief and chief executive, and there would be new editors in both the daily and the Sunday papers; these would be nominated by Denis Hamilton to the board, for their approval and appointment.

We had also to make a certain cash payment to the Astors, and Thomson Organisation agreed to buy the new Printing House Square office and lease it to the Times Newspapers Ltd. Of the stock of the new company Thomson Organisation would hold 85 per cent and the Astor Foundation 15 per cent. This ensured that our ownership could not at any time be assailed.

This deal was the greatest thing I had ever done. It was the summit of a lifetime's work. I had had to agree to keep out of the running of the paper; at least my son would be there sharing fully in its management. Yet, in spite of this sacrifice I was making, the takeover of *The Times* by the new company was immediately referred by the Prime Minister to a Monopolies Commission, as if the House of Commons had every right, which I didn't deny, to be suspicious of what we were up to.

On 27th October, 1966, Jim Coltart, Denis Hamilton, Gordon Brunton, Kenneth and I met the Commission. It consisted of Mr. A. W. Roskill, Q.C., chairman, a leading silk with some experience of parliamentary inquiries; Lord Annan, Provost of University College, London, and well-known broadcaster; Brian Davidson, a director of

the Bristol Aeroplane Company and a member of
Gloucester County Council; Professor B. S. Yamey, in
the chair of economics at University College, London;
Lord Francis-Williams, broadcaster and writer of a
column on the press and former editor of the *Daily
Herald*; W. E. Jones, former president of the National
Union of Mineworkers, and, until recently, chairman of
the Southern Regional Board; Edgar Richards, a stockbroker; and Donald Tyerman, recently retired from the
editorship of *The Economist* and at one time an assistant
editor of *The Times*. A formidable team, not likely to be
put off their purpose, which was to find out whether the
new company taking over *The Times* was going to be
mindful of its traditions or was going to run it in such a
way as would not be in the public interest.

In many ways it was farcical to suggest that this
commission would serve any useful purpose. We were
the only people who could save *The Times*. Whatever
Lord Astor might think about my not being on the board,
and whatever device we might adopt to give the new
company a very respectable public image, there was no
doubt the people who could save the newspaper itself
were the highly skilled marketing, advertising and
editorial men who belonged to the Thomson Organisation and would have the full use of the organisation's
resources and services.

I understand that John Wyndham, who was Harold
Macmillan's private secretary during his long and distinguished prime-ministership, had got together a
consortium of moneyed men prepared to invest in taking
over *The Times*. They hadn't the faintest hope of making
a success of the paper (nor indeed would the Astors have
given them the chance) for they knew nothing about the
newspaper business; they were in fact hopelessly devoid
of the very qualities that *The Times* itself had been short
of, which were the skills and the expertise only we could

give to the paper. So it was really silly that these good men of the commission should be required to spend so much time investigating us to see if we would 'do'. For this, explicitly, was their commission: they had to seek out whether the arrangements we would be making for 'their' paper would be commendable in the tradition of *The Times*, whether we had appointed or would appoint the right kind of men to run it, and whether we would guarantee it its independent voice. It was as if, at the end of my working life, I was being put on trial by the decision of the English Establishment to see whether I and my money were worthy of their trust to the extent of being allowed to take care of their leading Establishment paper, the paper that the 'top people' read.

This feeling of being on trial persisted right through the first long day of questioning, and again during the second day, a month later, when we all (except Kenneth, who had to be in Canada) came back to it again. Not once but many times I told them that I was only taking on *The Times* because I reckoned its rescue and restoration to health would be a worthy object and perhaps a fitting object for a man who had made a fortune out of newspapers. I knew, I said, that I was going to lose a lot of money before *The Times* became viable again, and if it ever did become a profitable concern, it would very likely never repay the big sums, the millions, we would have to invest in it. We knew that, my son and I, yet we were prepared to devote a large amount of our private fortune to this end. There was no question about that. Kenneth was as keen as I was, now that we saw we had been given the chance to save *The Times* and to take it under the wing of our organisation.

It would be our money that would be lost, I assured them, not anybody else's. The financial arrangement was that in the first place *The Times* losses would be shouldered by the *Sunday Times*. If the *Sunday Times* were to make too little profit in any one year to cover those losses, then my son and I would forgo enough of the dividends which would be due to us on our 78 per cent holding of Thomson Organisation shares. This would leave the outside shareholders of the organisation untouched. To make this a fool-proof arrangement, Thomson Scottish Associates, a company which derived its income wholly from Thomson Organisation and from which my son and I got our private fortune in Britain, gave an official company guarantee to cover *The Times* losses. This I read out to the commission and their shorthand writers:

'With a view to ensuring continual publication of *The Times* and the *Sunday Times* as newspapers with complete editorial independence, we, Thomson Scottish Associates Limited, undertake to procure that, to the extent that the same cannot be provided by Times Newspapers Limited, the Thomson Organisation or other sources, the necessary means will be made available to Times Newspapers to enable them to continue publishing these papers as quality papers edited in the national interest. This undertaking will continue for twenty-one years and will be binding on our successors and assigns.'

This was a company undertaking and not a personal one for the simple reason that, if it had been my guarantee and not the company's, my will couldn't have been settled for twenty-one years and the same could have happened to my son. The company undertaking in fact put everything in our British estate behind the continuation of *The Times*.

Put simply this meant that if the profits of the *Sunday Times* failed to carry the losses of *The Times*, and the Thomson Organisation could not carry those losses without their ordinary dividend being affected, then our Scottish company could use the resources coming to them from our 78 per cent of the Organisation dividends without affecting the dividends paid to the other Organisation shareholders.

All this investment in the future of *The Times* was something beyond the limits of normal business. We were injecting more than an ordinary kind of private enterprise investment into the paper—we were setting no limit to the money we were prepared to put into it, and we were asking no guarantees about ever getting it back. I would not have been willing to do this for any other newspaper or any other purpose. I told the commission that I was doing it simply out of a profound belief that *The Times* must be saved. To save *The Times* we must put the kind of money into it that would carry it through, without any strings attached or restrictions applied, and my son had agreed with me. If it was a bad investment we must accept that. We could afford this one impulse of generosity, this one extravagance. The transcript says that I added, 'I would not do that ordinarily.' That was surely a choice understatement.

We expected to lose over a million in the first year, and we told the commission that we might have to provide five million before we could pull *The Times* into a position of viability. With any other paper we would not have considered it, for that kind of money would take a long time to come back, if it ever did. But we conceived it as our duty, Ken and I, to do a good and unstinted job on this project. And I was greatly moved that my son never questioned my decision, and wholeheartedly agreed with me in pouring away all those millions to save an ideal.

This was the way my life had come to a final purpose; it was my destiny, if you can take such a grand word. I had made a big fortune through radio and television and newspapers, and now I was being given, or expected to be given, the chance of saving this fine old English newspaper. I was not going to duck that.

175

We had also to give undertakings that neither ourselves individually nor the Thomson Organisation in its
corporate entity would interfere in the editorial policy
and independence of *The Times* or the *Sunday Times*.
Denis Hamilton, too, as future editor-in-chief, had to give
assurances that the editors of the two papers would be
responsible for the editorial opinions of the papers, and
that these two men would be free to put forward opposing
views. The commission was very concerned about this,
having in their minds the long history of independence
which *The Times* editor had enjoyed. I see from the
commission's report that I spelled it out very fully and
plainly for them and they quoted what I said in their
report. I believe it is worth repeating:

'Denis Hamilton and I have worked closely together
since I appointed him editor of the *Sunday Times* in
1961, and we frequently talk together. I have views on
various subjects and I make sure that he knows them,
but I never see them in the paper unless he agrees with
them. We discuss things, and he knows that I am very
concerned in my mind about certain things, but he is the
editor and nothing of my views goes into the paper unless
they are also his views. No newspaper today, and I think
we must recognize this, can operate with an editor in
isolation. A newspaper is a very big business proposition. Someone has to decide "How much money can we
afford to spend?" on an editorial department or any other
department. These are matters which have to be decided
on a high level basis . . . I am satisfied that he would be
the best editor for *The Times*, but I think it is too big a
job for a man to be editor of both papers. I think there
must be an editor of *The Times* and an editor of the
Sunday Times and I think they must both make their own
decisions, as Mr. Hamilton has said, in the final analysis.
I think they need a lot of assistance and advice, and I
think, if they are the type of people that I hope they will

be, they will want to seek advice as Mr. Hamilton seeks it from me occasionally, but he does not observe it unless he sees fit to carry it out. I believe he will be a tower of strength to these editors . . . '

This was backed up by a further guarantee that if the editor of either paper felt that any outside interests in which the Thomson Organisation was concerned deserved adverse comment in the columns of *The Times* or of the *Sunday Times* he would be entirely free to express that comment, and in doing so would have the complete protection of Denis Hamilton. This was coming to the question of the octopus, and what people thought of as the vast amorphous organisation that we had built up and how it spread its tentacles everywhere, and didn't these tentacles threaten the independent life of the subsidiaries?

I gave the commission some relevant and useful figures. An analysis of the circulation figures of the national and provincial papers showed that IPC had 36·8 per cent of the total for the country, Beaverbrook had 18·1 per cent, and Associated Newspapers 10·9. We, with *The Times* included, would have 6·5 per cent, which did not seem dangerously near being a monopoly. With the addition of *The Times* we would have only a third of Beaverbrook's circulation. If the analysis was confined to quality papers, we would have 40 per cent of the Sunday circulation, and of the daily figures, with *The Times* included, only 12 per cent. These were the great monopolistic inroads that we were proposing to make into the newspaper world.

At the end of the second day, this is what I said to the commission:

'This is the most difficult task that we have ever accepted. It is going to be a very big job to carry it through. We cannot do it, we will never accomplish it, if there are any handicaps placed in our way. As a matter of fact, if there are, I will not even undertake it, because it would be a hopeless proposition. I hope that, in any recommendations you make, you will have that in mind.'

This, as I read it now, was pretty bluntly telling them where they, or Parliament to whom they had to report, stood. Well, they did not waste time. Before the end of the year (1966) they produced a fifty-page report for Parliament. It repeated all the pledges we had given them and this was the conclusion of seven of them, Mr. Brian Davidson dissenting:

'The evidence of our witnesses showed that the proposed transfer has aroused apprehensions for the public interest and our investigations have suggested that these apprehensions are not groundless. The independence of *The Times* could not be regarded as certain, and it must be recognized that if it came under the control of the Thomson Organisation commercial considerations would play a greater part than they have in the past. But in the light of the Thomson Organisation's assurances about its intentions for the paper's management . . . we think that there is every prospect that the survival of *The Times* would be assured, that the public would continue to be offered a good, and in some respects an improved, newspaper, and moreover in matters of editorial opinion there is reasonable assurance that it would continue to speak with a separate voice. It would no longer be the same voice or the same *Times* as in the past, and it is important that it should be recognized, both at home and abroad, that it would have no claim to any special role or status; but we do not regard that as contrary to the public interest . . . But we think that neither [the] increase in competitive strength nor the increase in concentration of ownership which would result from the proposed transfer is, of itself, cause for concern.'

Mr. Davidson, for his part, could not avoid the conclusion that the transfer of *The Times*, 'which immediately has much to commend it, might operate against the public interest. I think that the admitted difficulty in devising fully satisfactory protective measures does not invalidate this conclusion.'

So the transfer took place.

William Rees-Mogg, who was then deputy editor of the *Sunday Times*, became editor of *The Times*, and Harold Evans, whom Denis Hamilton had brought a year or so earlier for just such a possible eventuality from Darlington, where he had been editor-in-chief of the *Northern Echo* group, took over the editorship of the *Sunday Times*.

The first chairman of the newly-formed company, Sir William Haley, threw himself unselfishly and dynamically into the business of making the merger work and I shall always be grateful to him, and to the first national directors, Lord Shawcross, Lord Robens, Sir Eric Roll and Sir Donald Anderson. Gavin Astor has remained president with my son and the continuing interest of the Astor family in *The Times*, offering every possible help and backing, has been greatly appreciated by older members of the staff and of great assistance to the new regime.

Thomson Organisation men had not been long in Printing House Square before they realized how inadequate the new building was as an office for a daily paper of the size and importance of *The Times*, the staff of which would now have, in any case, to be increased. We had the editorial spread over three floors. If we were to bring the production of the two newspapers together for economy and efficiency, so that they could be printed on the same machinery and share many of the same services, then it would have to be at Gray's Inn Road, in a new building erected on the vacant site adjoining Thomson House, to house *The Times* with all its staff and ancillary services properly and to concentrate *The Times* editorial staff on one floor. This move is now complete and anyone who cares to take note of the amount of space given to *The Times* in the new building next to the *Sunday Times* office will see we were left with no choice. The building at Printing House Square opposite Blackfriars Station had to be sold and the New Printing House Square created in Gray's Inn Road. Thankfully, it was found possible to preserve the name.

In this period, too, we worked hard to build up the *Sunday Times*—the paper often grew to 72 pp. and the Colour Magazine to 96. In the year after the merger we had reached a sale of 1,500,000 and, in spite of a five-fold increase in price, we have managed to maintain this remarkable figure. Some years there has been a reasonable profit return on the heavy investment involved but we have had to struggle constantly against being swamped by rising production and newsprint costs.

It seems no time at all, but eight years of running *The Times* have passed into the ledgers and the balance sheets and into the index since Times Newspapers Ltd. was formed to take it over. They have been anxious years, and exciting years too, when *The Times* found its new feet and started to compete more vigorously with its contemporaries, especially in marketing its advertising potential. The losses sustained from one year to the next have been formidable. In eight years my son and I have given up well over eight millions of our private fortune to fill the gaps. Have we been mad?

The debit balance from one year to another has dwindled. The paper can be viable if the staff continue to back us, and if we are able to bring in more automation. This does not mean that in future years I will see all those millions coming back to us out of the profits. I doubt if, even after I am long gone, Ken will ever see that money. Maybe his son will. David, my grandson, will have to take his part in the running of the Organisation, and David's son, too. For the business is now all tied up in trusts for those future Thomsons, so that death duties will not tear it apart.

With the fortune that we will leave to them go also responsibilities. These Thomson boys that come after Ken are not going to be able, even if they want to, to shrug off these responsibilities. The conditions of the trusts ensure that control of the business will remain in Thomson hands for eighty years.

11

THE BROTHERS IN DISUNION

IN JANUARY 1967 I had the nerve to tell the House of Lords what I thought was wrong with the British press. The debate followed the publication of the Report on the Press by the Economist Intelligence Unit which had investigated the workings of a number of London newspapers on behalf of the Joint Board for the Newspaper Industry (representing both unions and proprietors). What I said then I have repeated in full in the appendix at the back of this book for anyone who may be interested, for it is all still valid and there is another inquiry into the press now being held, this time by a Royal Commission, and they, I dare say, will come up with the same home truths. But I'm afraid they may not be so optimistic in their conclusions as I was in 1967. The industry has, in recent years, gone through some pretty harsh experiences, particularly in its industrial relations. I have had some experiences myself in that field, and I suppose I must have lost some of my blithe Canadian optimism when I start thinking about the industry's labour problems.

As I have explained in a previous chapter, I had the idea in 1966 of introducing into this country the North American practice of producing an evening paper that serves a much smaller community than is reckoned possible in Britain. This kind of paper, since it can have only a small circulation, is viable only if it is produced with advanced technology and many fewer operatives. A really local newspaper produced daily is—or was before we started—virtually unknown in this country in communities of a size comparable with those in the States and in Canada which enjoy and maintain profitably an evening paper of their own with a circulation that is often less than 20,000 and not much more than 15,000. That, they assured me, simply could not be done in England, not with the wage-bill we would have.

How can it be done in America and not here? I will tell you.

I knew all about over-manning and the prohibitive cost of labour, machines and materials. I fondly believed that I could overcome these difficulties. I knew that there were around London, in the densely populated south-east of England, a string of towns that were important enough commercially and in the size of their populations and not only because they were satellite towns in the great sprawling conurbation of London. I knew that towns like Watford and Luton and St. Albans were receiving editions of the *Evening Standard* and the *Evening News* that had to be printed early in the day to get to their destinations in time, and moreover that very few businesses or private individuals in those towns could afford to advertise in a London evening paper. So I had the situation thoroughly studied and came to the conclusion that it would be worth while to ring London with a chain of local evening papers. With the new technology, with the unions induced to accept low manning levels in order to create more jobs, and with the advanced know-how and skills of our organisation applied to selling local advertising, I knew that the heavy investment in machinery would be handsomely repaid. It could have been done but it wasn't.

G 183

If I am to be blunt about this and tell anything resembling the truth of a very complicated affair, so that others may be warned or may learn how to make progress, I can only say this: we were beaten by the unions. The two mainly involved, the NGA and NATSOPA, were both willing to agree to the principle of economical manning so that new papers could be started and new jobs secured for their members. In other words, they agreed to forgo the traditional union 'blow' system whereby thousands of men in the press and dispatch departments of newspapers throughout Fleet Street work with a very generous system of rest periods and thereby force the management to take on many more staff than necessary. The two unions accepted that if Fleet Street manning levels were applied in Hemel Hempstead there was no possibility of starting the two new evening papers.

But then, as I have said, that old shibboleth of the printers, the differentials of the craft union, raised its hoary head and blocked us. For the new web-offset machines had to have men from both unions, and separating the work of one lot from the other would have been very difficult if not impossible. But the NGA, with its pride in its history as a craft union, would have stopped, and for a time did stop, the whole enterprise rather than admit their working brothers of NATSOPA to equality of status. They would have allowed hundreds of men to lose their jobs and their futures at Hemel rather than permit a 'machine minder' to do any simple task that should have been done by a 'machine manager'. The men from NATSOPA were not to be allowed to undertake certain 'craft' functions, not because they wouldn't have been able to perform these fairly simple jobs, but because the particular tasks had been from time immemorial the prerogative of the NGA. Perhaps not unnaturally the other union were equally inflexible in demanding that this old prerogative could not be regarded as everlasting and that their men were not going to go on for ever accepting a second-class role.

One can see some reason also in the NGA attitude if one looks back into the history of printing newspapers. Small unions have been swamped by big ones, and some craftsmen have lost their distinction as such because their functions in the industry and even their departments have been lost in a dilution by unskilled or semi-skilled labour. But today the unions have to face something a great deal more crucial than these nice distinctions and demarcation problems. Today they have to look not to their traditions in the past but to the overwhelming changes facing them in the future. With the new technology these changes are bound to sweep right through the industry.

The revolution in machines and methods is now spreading across North America. It is transforming the industry there faster than the linotype machine did when it took over the tasks of the old compositors, laboriously setting by hand, and made the modern newspaper possible.

This time the revolution springs from the use of the computer which we brought to work at Reading and Hemel Hempstead with a bit of a struggle, as I have recounted. But the rate of progress in the new techniques since computer-setting was first introduced in America fifteen years ago has been breathtaking. From original computer-assisted setting producing 150 lines of type per minute, new machines have been brought out that deliver one thousand lines a minute, six columns wide, in sheets for photo-composition. A man then cuts them into the shapes required by the page design, pastes them in position, the page is photographically transferred to a plastic plate which is then wound round the cylinder for printing.

All our old systems are being transformed. Copy is typed on electric typewriters and scanned by machines called Optical Character Readers which translate it into punched tape, or it is set on the keyboard of a Video Display Terminal which is combined with a cathode ray tube screen on which the setting is shown and on which the computer will immediately show any line or paragraph or column that is wanted for correction or sub-editing and these functions are performed by a simple use of the keyboard. This keyboard, they say, can be used 'even by a reporter or sub-editor'—and in North America it is in fact so used.

This is a clear indication of the scale of this revolution or what it may become when in full swing. Old skills are being dispensed with, whole departments are no longer needed. In a Detroit evening paper office reporters don't sit battering old typewriters but take their places at Video Display Terminals to send their stories straight into the computer. From the computer the news editor recalls the story he wants to read on to the screen of his V.D.T. and by using his keyboard he can alter what he wants to alter. The story then passes on from the computer to the chief sub-editor's screen (it can, of course, be on several screens simultaneously) and thence to a sub-editor for final correction and cutting before it goes to the plant on the outskirts of the city, either as a photograph for photo-composition or as hot metal by tele-typesetting machine if it is late news. It can, if they are pushed for time, be in the page twenty miles away fifteen minutes after the reporter sits down at his V.D.T.

Other giant steps have followed. The profitable morning paper in Miami, the *Miami Herald*, sets fifty pages of classified advertising every day. The girls, who sell and take these ads. by telephone, type them electrically and feed them straight as they come into the computer. These are corrected on V.D.T. screens and type sizes marked. They are disgorged a column at a time by the computer, which itself arranges them in correct order and in

186

groups according to classification, cars for sale, secretaries wanted and so on. It is reckoned that seven man-hours are needed to produce a page of these ads., including the time of the girls taking them down on the phone. A page of such ads. in a British newspaper today would take at least twenty man-hours in setting and composing by the traditional methods.

In some American offices the editorial now attend to the composing of their own pages. Why give the job to someone else to do when the page-designer has only to cut lengths of photo-setting and fit them into his plan? And there are machines that, using a simple keyboard, set headlines that fit the right width by contracting or widening the characters.

The changes are being accepted gradually in union houses all over North America because American union men recognize the grim alternative facing them. What else can save their newspapers from having to close down as they had to close down in New York? There the struggle between unions and management was so protracted that the unimaginable happened and there are now only four papers daily, including the financial paper, compared with the eleven, morning and evening, that still come out in London.

But in London, what is happening? An attempt to introduce computer setting was first made by the *Evening Standard* but it failed: the employees wouldn't have it. The first breakthrough was at *The Times*, but the equipment put into operation there is grossly under-used. Later the *Financial Times* succeeded in introducing a limited amount of computer-assisted setting. At *The Times* we were also the first (in London) to operate photo-typesetting but not by any means as widely as we would have wished. There were two insuperable difficulties. First, we couldn't get the right kind of operators on to the keyboards; it would generally be a lot easier to train a typist than to retrain a linotype operator for this work, but you can guess how popular we would be if we tried to employ women (as is done in Russia) in the mechanical end of the newspaper industry in the en-lightened and sex-liberated 1970s. In any case, the second obstacle was enough in itself: that was the London scale of payments, the piece-workers' bible, which was entirely inappropriate to computer-assisted photo-setting, but had to be applied with no adjustments, so we were faced with costs that again blocked progress.

After we had invested £2,500,000 in the two-paper project at Hemel Hempstead, we were prevented from using our new machines and the most advanced tech-niques in Britain (if not, at that time, in the world) because the NGA insisted they had an absolute right to craft jobs even if those jobs no longer required craft. It looked like the end of 600 jobs (at today's count) until the TUC, prodded by the Hemel Hempstead workers parading in protest against the union action, and stirred up also by Eric Cheadle, the Thomson Organisation deputy managing director, found a formula to which both unions agreed, although they made it plain, so very plain, that this was an agreement exclusive to Hemel Hemp-stead and that it must not be taken to create a precedent for anywhere else. Eric Cheadle asked for formal agree-ments to be drawn up between the two unions and en-dorsed by the TUC. All he ever got was a letter from Vic Feather telling him what had been agreed. Only in the last resort, and only to stop all these people being turned out of their jobs as a direct consequence of a demarcation dispute, had the unions agreed that their men could work together. They had done this only because they had been pressurized into agreement by the TUC, who had been appalled at the bad publicity the trade-union move-ment was getting from the Hemel Hempstead dispute.

The story of what happened at Belfast as a consequence

of the Hemel clash may be liable to different interpretations. This is how I heard it at the time:

Prompted by Eric Cheadle, who was, as I have said, a friend of Vic Feather, then George Woodcock's deputy, the TUC special committee which was investigating the demarcation dispute at Hemel decided to send a deputation to Belfast where the International Publishing Corporation had begun the printing of the *Daily Mirror* Northern Ireland edition on a web-offset machine similar to our machines at Hemel and in Belfast the two unions were apparently manning the machine quite harmoniously.

In the Belfast press-room, the London delegates clambered all over the machine talking to the men who were operating it and were apparently a little taken aback when neither the NGA men nor the NATSOPA men could clearly differentiate their duties. They were all Ulstermen, who had worked in provincial offices and were now in a national office enjoying national pay, and their only thought was to do whatever had to be done to get the paper out on time. Among the delegates were Mr. Bonfield of the NGA and Mr. Briginshaw of NATSOPA, and one wonders what their reactions were to what they saw in Belfast, where there had been a good deal of flexibility between jobs. It was, however, directly due to that visit and to the conversation on the plane between Messrs. Cooper, Woodcock, Feather and Bonfield, that a purely local and not-to-be-repeated arrangement between the two unions was contrived for Hemel Hempstead to get the new papers going and prevent hundreds of people being paid off.

The irony was that soon afterwards some sort of dispute on a demarcation point broke out at Belfast, where, prior to the deputation's visit, men of the two unions had been working together in brotherly amity. Whether this dispute, which stopped printing of the *Daily Mirror* in Belfast, was a result of that visit of the TUC delegation

189

reminding the Belfast men of their union loyalties is a matter for conjecture. Later the print-works was extensively damaged by an I.R.A. bomb and IPC decided they had had enough. They abandoned the Belfast printing and the newspaper industry shrank a little more as a result.

One of the great sadnesses of my working life is that the unions in the printing industry have never been able to get together, to establish one union and a real brotherhood. It is true that NATSOPA and the Print-workers formed a joint union called SOGAT but that soon broke apart at the seams. True, NGA is an amalgam of compositors, machine managers, stereotypers, readers and press telegraphists, but this has never created a flexibility or interchangeability that one would expect from a single-union situation. I understand that there are again discussions between a number of unions about joining forces, and I very much hope that this will lead to the day when there is one union in the industry with full interchangeability, so that a man by his own endeavours may gain promotion from one grade to another. I don't know how a man feels when he knows he is stuck in a groove for the whole of his life; I couldn't have taken that. Real flexibility in the industry would also bring economies to the operation of newspapers and the chance of greater job-security.

I have always been impressed by the high standard of intelligence of the officers of the printing unions and likewise of the men on the shop floor. People I talk to who have experience in several industries tell me that the average of intelligence in the printing industry is far higher than in other industries. Perhaps this is why I find it so galling that the people in the newspaper industry don't clearly see the facts of life and the urgent need for a basic change of attitudes.

After our brush with NGA and NATSOPA at Hemel Hempstead, we felt we had to shrink our plans a little as

IPC had done at Belfast, and except for a joint operation in Slough, abandon the project of starting further evening papers around London. There may have been some additional reason for this but certainly the complete intractability of the unions, their stubborn refusal to offer us any hope of applying the new technology elsewhere so that we could make our enterprise economic, had taken a lot of steam out of the project. It had begun to have a very risky look.

This is the pity of it. The new technology will come to the help of the industry sooner or later. But it will come too late, I fear, to save some of the papers which are already finding survival a hard struggle. So the reduction in the number of jobs in the industry will go on while the new techniques are kept waiting, and when the revolution comes to the industry, when the big changes are made, it will not be so easy to make them without hurting people.

Fortunately I had plenty of other things to think of besides my disagreements with the unions and my failure to get across to them the warning I hoped they would one day heed.

At the start of these twenty years in Britain, I tried to give the *Scotsman* (and its proprietor) more friendly connections and influence among important people of Scotland by frequently holding luncheons and dinners so that these people could get to know me and my chief assistants and learn through their conversation with us what our real purpose was for the paper. And when I found myself with the *Sunday Times* under my control I developed and greatly extended the same practice in London.

Entertaining important guests from all areas of public life at Thomson House became a very vital part of my weekly routine from 1962 onwards, and we took great care that these lunches would be successful, that our V.I.P.

guest speakers would feel they had not wasted their time and that the other guests would be glad that they had come. We usually had between twenty and twenty-four people round the board-room table, and we tried to keep formality to a minimum. After the chief guest had spoken, there was always about thirty minutes' discussion. I could always have at the table one or two of our leading journalist experts in the field in which the speaker was concerned, so that he might be drawn out by questioning to make perhaps some significant addition to what he had said, and sometimes we had some good-going arguments.

Among the chief guests who graced our table and took part in these off-the-record talks were the Duke of Edinburgh, all the Prime Ministers of the period, many Cabinet Ministers, City men, industrialists, trade-union leaders, academics and writers. We did not do things by halves. There were always printed guest lists and place-cards, printed menus with the list of previous chief guests and speakers. I always gave to each person as they left one of the most handsome books recently put out by one of our book-publishing companies. You may be surprised to know how much this little gesture contributed to the success of these weekly lunches, for even a multi-millionaire financier likes a free book to take home, especially those on gardening or history.

When we saw that our hospitality was appreciated we extended it to dinners, especially for V.I.P.s visiting England, and often, too, when some important issue was exercising the country, such as the Common Market or the Atlantic alliance. We helped in this way to spread ideas among men of influence and to bring opposing opinions closer together.

Not, of course, that we could do that with a forceful character like Lord George-Brown. He was our chief guest when he was Foreign Secretary and took the opportunity to attack me because we were serializing in the *Sunday Times* the highly dramatic discoveries we had made in the course of brilliantly executed investigations into the hitherto unknown activities and associations of the spy Philby. George Brown said we were doing great damage by making these revelations. But Denis Hamilton told me afterwards that the editor of the *Sunday Times* had taken steps to see that anything that could possibly endanger the present members of MI6 would not be printed and that every line had been most assiduously vetted.

This, curiously enough, was not the only attack I had to suffer from George. On the other occasion I had him as my chief guest at a dinner I gave a company of American businessmen, and George, having arrived very late, accused me outright of having cheated him, referring to the fact that I didn't put up the money to rescue Upper Clyde Shipbuilders, as he had hoped or expected I would. Somehow one always forgave George, though his behaviour at public functions was unpredictable.

One lunch I gave to a very famous American industrialist had an amusing moment. He had obviously travelled overnight from the Caribbean, where he had big interests, and could not stop himself from dozing in his chair as soon as he had finished eating. We were discussing the American dilemma over Vietnam and one of the guests, Field-Marshal Montgomery, was questioning the wisdom of the U.S. presence on the mainland of Asia. My guest woke up with a start at that moment.

'I will not have my country's motives attacked by a British admiral,' he said.

We all looked at Monty. He was doubled up with laughter.

I was always particularly glad to invite to my table a leader from one of the developing countries. There was, in fact, scarcely a day in my working life when I was not visited by someone from Africa or Asia looking for news of new techniques, of new methods of raising revenue, or for advice about setting up newspapers or magazines in their own countries. I tried to see all of them. A few years ago a young student walked into my office for a talk—without any introduction—and I gave him what advice I could. I saw that he had exceptional talents. He is now High Commissioner for Kenya in London.

In these countries the press itself has a big part to play in the modernizing process in which they are all vitally engaged and that process does demand continual contact with the Western world and its thinking. But I am afraid that in some Asian and African countries there are many subtle ways of exercising an influence and restraint on the so-called free press: through licensing of newspapers and the threat of loss of licence, through rationing of newsprint, through many unseen but effective pressures brought upon publishers and editors. One sanction was applied to one of our Africa papers which had injudiciously criticized the government and supported the opposition party. For many months after the incident the Minister of Information would approach one or other of our advertisers at a reception or cocktail party saying, 'I see you are donating funds to the opposition party.' When this was vigorously denied, he would explain, 'If you take advertising space in the —— it is as good as a donation to the party.' The effect on our revenue was instantaneous and serious.

Perhaps not unnaturally the biggest trouble of that kind we had in Africa was in Rhodesia. There we had taken over a small paper, which had been started to give the Africans a voice. It had not been much of a success, but the possibilities were there and we had turned it into the *African Daily News* and, under the editorship of Eugene Wason, it was flourishing. Now one thing that Eugene had laid down to his African assistants and contributors was that the paper would never tolerate any incitement to violent means of obtaining the share of power for the Africans; they must always advocate the winning of power by peaceful and constitutional means.

Suddenly there was an election and unexpectedly the National Front gained power, and one of the first things the new government did was to ban the *Daily News*, accusing it of being subversive. Gordon Brunton flew out at once to Salisbury and saw Lardner Burke, the African affairs minister, who told him bluntly that they wouldn't have the *News* published, it was too powerful. Gordon saw that Eugene Wason had been very near to arrest. He then went to see the President, Dupont.

Dupont told him he could restart the paper and he could be sure of commercial success if he would give a guarantee that he would only print what was approved by the government. Gordon came on to the telephone to me. He said he had been left in no doubt: he was being offered a bait. There would be a handsome profit no doubt, but he didn't think I would like this move any more than he would. I said he was right and that we should pull out of Rhodesia. This we did, taking, of course, a heavy loss in the process.

Gordon has reminded me of these happenings, giving them as an example of how, more often than people realized, principle was put before profit by the Organisation.

In Africa there are some countries where there are no newspapers at all. In others the single newspaper is published in the capital under full governmental control. In those few countries where there are independent papers the influence of the government is still strong. African leaders such as President Nyerere contend that Western standards of press freedom are not right for developing countries of Africa. He believes that newspapers are part of the modernizing process but for this reason they should be run under government control.

I have explained that when Prime Minister Balewa of Nigeria was being upset by the critical nature of our editorials, he told me when I visited Nigeria to see what was in his mind: 'If you are to operate a newspaper in my country, you must always realize that what the African reads in print he believes to be gospel. At the same time I need your newspaper and you are at liberty to criticize our judgement and our methods, but you must do it objectively and try to help us always.'

It *is* important to realize the difference between the African and the British reader. The latter very often sees two or three different papers and is usually highly sceptical about what he reads. At the same time there is too great sensitivity among African politicians and sometimes a determination to conceal the facts from the outside world; expulsion of correspondents happens in too many places and too often. But the problems of political freedom are not as simple as they may seem.

It was with this in mind that we came to the conclusion that we must do something to share our knowledge in the operation of mass media. Without smoothly running information services, development in these countries would be retarded. So we decided in 1964 to set up the Thomson Foundation the purpose of which was, and is, to train senior men who have the responsibility for the operation of newspapers and television stations in new countries and developing countries throughout the world. We endowed this foundation with £5m., and James Coltart (now its chairman) has been the main architect of its work since the start. For all these years we have run advanced courses for newspapermen at our journalists' college in Cardiff, and in Scotland we have a residential training college for television and radio. In addition to these two colleges, which are in operation throughout the year, we send experts overseas to conduct training seminars. In our last three seminars in India we put through the concentrated courses journalists from over 38 newspapers.

In addition to the 500 senior journalists who have taken courses at Cardiff, men who operate news agencies in twenty countries have been given specialist training. While attending these courses our visitors learn how the British press is run and the part it plays, often behind the scenes, in British life and politics.

Besides these activities, we have given a great deal in the way of skills and experience and, in effect, loans to the under-developed countries by building and equipping for them new television stations, which we then run for five or ten years with a staff of our own specialists, producers, engineers and managers, till the local men are able to take over fully on their own. This we have done without profit in Kenya, Mauritius, Gibraltar, Sierra Leone, Ethiopia, Barbados, Jamaica, Bermuda and Pakistan. For these stations we purchased all the equipment, we trained the producers, and we carried on the business till it was running at a profit and they could take over.

There is an unexpected side-light on all this. We also train the British Army in television techniques. Officers from overseas as well as from Home Commands come regularly through our training courses. When I am looking on my TV set at incidents in Ulster, I know that many of these men owe their assurance and poise in front of the cameras partly to Thomson training. And in a tricky situation a good showing on TV doesn't do the army or the situation any harm.

12

OIL UNDER TROUBLED WATERS

Y GREATEST asset, possibly, has been that, in my everyday life since I came to Britain, I have gone out of my way to meet and to get to know a lot of people. Because I have few inhibitions I have been able freely to make friends with all manner of people, people who have sought me out in my office or whom I have met at luncheons and official receptions and public dinners. Many of my friends think that I talk a lot, but I can also get others to talk. I think I proved this with Khrushchev and others equally eminent, but I didn't confine my gregariousness and natural curiosity to the top ranks. I never counted it wasted time to meet someone new, however important or unimportant he might appear to be. I believed something could always be learned from a stranger.

In my office I have always made myself accessible; I have always insisted upon this, to the extent often of not allowing my staff, or of not waiting for them, to vet strangers who came to see me before permitting them to come into my office. It is surprising the things that have sprung from this, the surprising things I've learned.

I am always curious, always hopeful. I still often duck out of an office meeting to see what some visitor looks like and to find out what he wants. Likewise, I take quite a few telephone calls if my secretary happens to be busy or out of the room for the moment; I have told the switchboard that if there is no one of my personal staff to answer a call, to put it straight through to me. I don't want any information or opportunity to go elsewhere just because no one could take a call.

I try to make friends wherever I go and it is my fond belief that I usually succeed. The way I look at it, everyone has an idea and one in a dozen may be a good idea. If you have to talk to a dozen people to get one good idea, even just the glimmering of an idea, that isn't wasteful work. People are continually passing things on to me, because I have given them to believe that I will be interested, I might even pay for it! Sometimes, usually when it is least expected, something comes up that is touched with gold.

Abdul Al-Ghazzi was one of those. He was an Iraqi and he came in and talked to me about oil, oil in the Persian Gulf. He seemed to me a pretty knowledgeable character, and he wasn't talking big, he wasn't trying to impress me unduly, or to sell me something. He wanted me to help him, but he thought we might help each other, using what he called my prestige and his know-how.

I didn't laugh at him—hadn't young Roy Thomson gone in to see local big-wigs, seeking a chance like this?—and, because I took a liking to him, I promised to see him if ever I got to the Gulf. It was Abdul who later introduced me to the Gulf sheikhs, and through this I made a valuable contact with Dr. Armand Hammer of Occidental Oil.

In the Persian Gulf the British Foreign Office acted in what can only be called an unpredictable fashion. At this time they had given oil concessions to Um al Quwayne and to Sharjah, two of the Trucial emirates in the Gulf, specifying clearly that the concession applied only to the three-mile off-shore limit. The Sheikh of Sharjah, however, acting unilaterally, took twelve miles in plotting his concession and the Foreign Office did nothing to stop him. They had committed themselves to a course of action and would not enforce the three-mile limit. This, owing to the topography of the place, rendered negative the important part of the concession to Um al Quwayne, and this concession the Sheikh had already leased to Occidental Oil. The Americans had found favourable conditions for oil by seismograph, but while they were seeking to enlist the support of the Foreign Office to move Sharjah, learned that the British had withdrawn from the Gulf altogether a day before they were due to leave. In that day Iran stepped in and grabbed the off-shore islands. Britain did nothing about that either. In fact they completely failed to carry out their obligations.

Dr. Hammer came to see me, not being able to under-stand what the British Government were doing, and I went to see Michael Stewart and later Sir Alec Douglas-Home. By this time, of course, in the way these things work, it was already too late. We had withdrawn from the Gulf and that was that. But the least I could do then was to go out and see the two sheikhs involved whom I knew. The matter is still being negotiated, and Dr. Hammer was grateful for my help.

This was how I got to know really well the head of the big Occidental company and how, in March 1971, when I was approached to join the North Sea oil consortium that Dr. Hammer had formed I was at once eager to do so.

The approach was made to me by Henry Grunfeld of S. G. Warburg's. As a matter of fact I had introduced Henry to Dr. Hammer at a luncheon I gave for the American, but Warburg's had had a working relation-ship with Occidental for many years. That spring they were informed by the oil company of the formation of a group with Paul Getty and Allied Chemical to bid for a licence to drill in the North Sea. Occidental were anxious to include a British partner, preferably one with close Scottish connections, and there was little time left, for bidding was due to take place in April, and it was vital that Warburg's should find them such a partner within two or three weeks. They proposed to carry themselves an estimated $1m. in pre-award expenses but that each partner should bear its proportion of the $25m. cost of the actual exploration programme.

Warburg's first put out feelers to some Scottish investment houses but soon learned that Occidental were indeed a late-comer to the North Sea project and that most, if not all, of the investment trusts and institutions were by then already committed to other groups. Warburg's then turned their thoughts to interesting a commercial enterprise with a particularly Scottish background in what at that time could only be described as a highly speculative venture. Who could be more suitable for this enterprise than Roy Thomson? He owned the *Scotsman*, one of his principal companies was Thomson Scottish Associates, and as he had so often said, his name was spelt without a 'p'. I was also known, by Warburg's, to be a friend of Armand Hammer's. Henry Grunfeld rang me up on 1st March, 1971, and suggested that this might be the sort of venture that would attract me. I immediately agreed and was as amused as Henry was, having introduced him to Armand Hammer, now to have him introduce the oil man to me as a business partner. On 5th March, only a week after Occidental had got in touch with them, Warburg's held a preliminary meeting in their office with me and my two financial directors, Fred Cusk and Gerry Hamill, at the end of which I was able to say that I was very interested in the proposal.

I was very happy to have been offered a partnership with these people; they were the kind of commercial leaders with whom I didn't mind linking the Thomson Organisation.

It was, of course, a 'wild cat' venture. It was wholly problematical where the oil was and whether or not the site we were given might be in the right place. Further, it meant 'wild catting' in some pretty stormy waters. Drilling was going to cost us $40,000 a day and we might drill all over the six areas given to us and find no oil in any of them, or not enough anyway to justify setting up a platform and a pipeline a hundred miles or more across the sea-bed to the Scottish mainland.

This was different from buying a newspaper. With a paper, if it turned out a stumer, you could at least find a customer and get some of your money back. With oil, if all your strikes were dry, you got nothing at all in return for your $40,000 a day. But, of course, if you struck it rich, the rewards could be substantial.

When I took the proposition to Gordon Brunton, I was, for the above reasons, very ready to make an arrangement which would protect the shareholders of the Organization, as we had done in the case of the losses of *The Times*. With the oil, the company that was concerned in the consortium was again Thomson Scottish Associates, in which Ken and I hold about 96 per cent of the stock, but I agreed that if we struck oil Thomson Scottish Associates would sell 90 per cent of their holding to the Organisation in return for whatever sums Thomson Scottish had been called upon by then to lay out. In other words, Thomson Organisation could come into a successful oil business without any risk at all. Instead of having a 96 per cent share in the oil holding, I and my family would then have little more than the 78 per cent which was the extent of our holding in the Organisation. If you ask me why I did this, I would say that I felt I owed it to my shareholders.

This oil investment was, of course, a gamble, and, in spite of what you may think, I am not a gambler. I have taken plenty of risks in my life, but they have always been carefully considered risks. My idea of luck is that it is an opportunity seized. You go through life looking for opportunities, and because you have managed to seize quite a few of them you will be called lucky by your friends. This opportunity in the wild North Sea was also carefully considered.

Armand Hammer had spent most of his life negotiating trading arrangements with the Russians, having become a friend of Lenin in the first years of the Revolution. Subsequently, when he intended to retire, he had been called in to help Occidental Oil of California, and he had built it up into a great international company, one of his successes being the discovery of oil in Libya. I reckoned that if I could afford to lose my stake in this new venture, I couldn't lose it in better company, and of course his two other associates, Paul Getty and Allied Chemical, neither being small fry, were of the same mind.

As it happened we struck oil in the third area where we started to drill, and found a well which will give us at least 640 million barrels. It is difficult to realize the extent of this one strike. It was put to me like this. The well would be as big as any in Texas bar one.

When we began to develop this enterprise, we had to form a company to operate it and, looking for someone to run this company, we asked ourselves what our particular contribution would be to the working of the consortium. One thing we were in the best position to see to was that the Scottish end of the operation didn't go wrong. Bringing our pipeline from the Piper Field and contributing our part to the spread of new industry in the North East of Scotland would involve us in many problems in an area predominantly agricultural, problems of local relations and safeguarding the countryside, perhaps of completely changing the life of the people. As it happened we had someone in the Organisation better equipped and by nature suited to do just this than anyone we might have found outside. Alastair Dunnett, editor and also managing director of the *Scotsman*, was hoping soon to give up the editorship, and he was a man who all his life, journalistic and political, had kept clear in his sights the aim of preserving and improving the quality of life in his beloved Scotland. Indeed it was known to us that he had during his career refused one or two very good offers to go and work in London because, for one reason, it meant leaving his homeland and abandoning his intense interest in the advancement of Scottish affairs.

But Alastair is and was realist enough to know that preserving that Scottish life at its best meant introducing to his country the benefits of the new technology, that further depopulation was not to be prevented just by digging holes in the ground for more coal. We saw it as a happy chance that such a man should be available and we were very pleased when he agreed to take over the chairmanship of the new company, especially as his planning for the future of the *Scotsman* and of Scotsman Publications when he should leave them was already well advanced and very promising.

One of his first acts in his new position was to organise a site for the receiving end of the oil pipe from Piper Field at Scapa Flow, where the operation could be carried out without causing any spoiling of amenities or interference with every-day life. Scapa Flow is a bit farther from the well and its production platform, which we are now preparing, than Aberdeen itself would be, but besides avoiding any amenity or living trouble it also provides a fine natural deep-water anchorage for the big oil tankers. It was used in the 1914–18 War by the Royal Navy as an operational base, offering the fleet all-the-year-around shelter and protection from all the devilment of the wicked North Sea (except, as it transpired, from U-boats) and it was there that the German fleet went after the surrender in 1918.

As you may have already gathered I am not one to hang back when it comes to going and looking at any good investments. So I have been out in the middle of that sea looking at how these fellows are getting on with my share of the 640 million barrels of oil it is reckoned we will get out of that first well. People who have no contact with the offshore oil business have simply no idea of the immense scale on which it works, the size of the machinery, the finance, the imagination and the risks taken, especially the risks, to which I am always on the alert. There are of course the risks of finding nothing and then the risks of not getting in the right kind of engineering and machinery to complete the job, and then, I suppose, some time along the oil route—although I hope not in the near future—the risk of not selling it profitably enough.

I was only a month off my eightieth birthday when I flew out with some of my colleagues to the *Ocean Victory* then drilling about 110 miles due east of the coast of Caithness. I had plenty of money sunk at that spot in the rock a mile and a half below the bottom of the sea, and there had been so much exciting news in the last year or more that I simply couldn't resist the notion of going and seeing how it was all being done.

We flew out by helicopter from Aberdeen, a journey which lasted over an hour until we came to rest on the deck of this enormous *Ocean Victory*, the semi-submersible drilling rig which found Piper Field on the very first well it ever drilled. You have to be pretty nimble to get about these floating monsters. Everything is a matter of going up steps or down steps.

The drill pipe is of section steel which screws together in great lengths as the drill pushes further and further into the rock to find if the oil is there. It was a pretty fair day when I was out but I wouldn't care much for it on some of the winter days on what the Americans called 'the meanest sea in the world'. There seems to be a lot of grease and slippery mud about—they use the mud for lubrication and for certain chemical processes in the drill pipe—and they carry so much of it in great sacks that there are trucks running about between the decks doing nothing but collecting and delivering loads of the stuff.

This specially prepared mud is circulating all the time from the drilling deck right down to the bottom of the hole where the drill is, and as it ascends it brings with it geological samples which are sorted out immediately by geologists in a special laboratory aboard the ship. They report by teleprinter to their home base and the results go into computers which seem to give a pretty accurate first impression of what the rock adds up to and whether it is oil-bearing or not. Bob MacAlister, the Californian who runs the Occidental activity in Britain, showed us a lot of these geological samples and explained how they were able to read their secrets. Fascinating! There is nothing like a professional expert doing his job, and in the oil business, with the money involved, these experts have developed and improved their methods to an astonishing proficiency.

Since that day, when I am lying in my bed and hear a storm blowing up, I think of these people out there in the middle of the North Sea doing the sort of job that no one in my world had ever heard of a few years ago, and working at it for twenty-four hours a day, seven days a week, whether the wind blows or not. I find it a pity when I read articles by young journalists or listen to media men on television who seem to be more concerned with the doomwatch aspect of these adventures than with the tremendous advantages in comfort and peace of living that can come to our people once we get this North Sea oil ashore. Certainly I don't want to see pollution happening in these parts but I know something of the remarkable extent to which oil men go in all parts of the world to abate pollution and to reduce it to proportions well within the expectation and the acceptability of decent civilized communities. It is good that there are numerous places of beauty and quietness which stand apart and to which people can go when they want to restore themselves, and I don't think that man has any right to foul up such places. I must say, however, that the places that look most beautiful to me are not empty and deserted but alive rather with plenty of contented people in good jobs and with good prospects, people who can spend their lives doing something useful that benefits us all. By the same standard I don't see anything necessarily ugly in the places where people work. Good buildings, good design and good landscaping are a sure indication of a prospering citizenship.

I hope this is what we get out of the oil business, especially in Scotland. There couldn't be a worse time to be trying to arrange finance for these huge and promising developments. It will take the long established banks some little time to develop the techniques of financing on the scale required by oil developments, and with the tightness of funds in a period of economic recession there are bound to be delays in getting on with the urgent task of bringing the oil ashore and putting it into the industrial system, especially if the process is going to be interrupted by unpredictable political decisions and undue interference.

Why, you may ask, do I go on seeking new opportunities like this at my time of life? I can assure you I don't feel that I might one day be short of money. But I simply cannot comprehend how anyone of my temperament can enjoy his leisure cultivating dahlias or buying racehorses. To do nothing more than that sort of thing is completely foreign to my nature. I have got to be doing some sort of work, and of course I wouldn't enjoy that work unless it were profitable.

Even my wife, if she had lived, couldn't, I think, have induced me to settle down to retirement, not if it had to be spent in leisure, although I am willing to believe that not all those people who say they do enjoy such a life are necessarily lying. My wife was interested in horse-racing—could you imagine a man like me taking to the life of an old-time English lord near Newmarket? For that you have to be bred and trained; I must say some fine specimens of that breeding have come my way.

But this is not to say that I don't enjoy the days I spend in my house near the village of Fulmer in Buckinghamshire, where I have much comfort provided by the same couple who have been with me since those days in Edinburgh, and much serenity, and the contentment, not given to everybody in my position, of being at ease. I keep my life there as simple as I wish. It is a comparatively modest house, where I could, I suppose, entertain four or five couples if I wanted to. I rarely entertain anyone nowadays except the members of my happily expansive family.

One great blessing that money has brought me in this house is an indoor swimming pool, which I have recently installed. Swimming has always been my favourite form of physical exertion and I can now enjoy it whenever I like, when, to a man of my sedentary habits and not insignificant dimensions, it is beneficial to take exercise without having to support my weight. One other advantage possessed by Alderbourne Arches is of being near enough to a station on the Underground line, so that I can travel most of the way to the office by train and without interruption read newspapers all the way in and out. For my reading at home I have a constantly augmented collection of over three thousand crime and detective novels, about a quarter of which I have not yet begun; these are what I read for relaxation and which, after balance sheets, I have confessed I find most absorbing.

Of course I know that one day, and it cannot be very far off, I shall have to say good-bye to this simple life. This does not worry me. I have already faced death once; that was in Canada when I was told I had to have an immediate operation for the removal of a growth. The prospect of coming to the end of the run didn't really bother me much then. I am pretty phlegmatic in this respect. Luckily the growth was found to be benign. I still had more to do apparently.

But now I am in the straight and the winning-post is within my sights. So, I suppose I shall one day, soon enough, be giving an account of everything I have done and looking for things that are to my credit, and will I be able to explain then how I happen to have been a happy man?

Appendix

WHAT IS WRONG WITH
THE BRITISH PRESS?

SPEECH BY Lord Thomson in the House of Lords,
January 1967, in the debate initiated by Lord Arran
following the publication of the Report on the Press
by the Economist Intelligence Unit which, on behalf of
the Joint Council for the Newspaper Industry, had investigated the workings of a number of London papers.
Referring to the Report, which had been endorsed by the
Council under its chairman, Lord Devlin, Lord Thomson
said:

'It is a devastating indictment of Fleet Street. Anyone
who reads it will come to that conclusion. Serious and
condemnatory, it has attracted relatively little criticism
from those concerned, and, beyond a few statements that
there are inaccuracies, I have seen no claims that challenge the general conclusions reached.

'It is my opinion that the statements made and the
conclusions reached are not only accurate in the main but,
as might be expected in a report of this kind, conservative. This Report was authorized by both the
proprietors and the unions. There was no pressure, no
indication from either side that the E.I.U. were to do other
than produce an absolutely unbiased report; they were
to give the facts and reach their conclusions without fear
or favour. I say that the Report is conservative because
I know that if a time-and-motion study were made it
would be proven that much greater efficiency could be

achieved, resulting of course in bigger savings. The number of men employed in Fleet Street is so large as to have no relationship to the amount of work required to be done. This has come about through the years as the result of union demands and proprietor capitulations. If a new piece of equipment is to be installed, before it is accepted —if it is accepted at all—irrespective of how many men are reasonably required, the union demands more, many more; so that no existing jobs can be eliminated and no savings can accrue to the publisher. That, in effect, completely frustrates plant modernization and the ability to become more efficient.

'The Report comments on wages. Some of these are certainly excessive—not in all departments, mostly in the production departments. But perhaps most interesting is the fact that, in the case of many production workers, the wages actually paid have little relationship to the basic wage. The amount called for by industrial agreements seems to be just a figure on which to hang the extras. When we appeared before the Shawcross Commission on the Press we were asked to submit figures for one production department of our business showing basic wages as compared with actual wages earned in one particular week. The basic wage was £15 1s. whereas, including all house payments and extras, the amount paid was £38 13s. per man, and that was in 1961. To work £15 into £38 you have to have some weird and wonderful house payments, and some weird and wonderful ways of calculating extras to be tacked on to regular wages. I want to see high wages in the industry but they must be tied to productivity.

'The Report criticizes some managements, and I am sure that anyone who has had experience of management techniques in other businesses or other countries would agree with those criticisms. It says that my own organisation and one other are efficient. I would say that we may

211

be efficient by British standards but not by good Canadian or American standards. Our directors and managers are very able men, and they operate our business as efficiently as possible. But how can we be really efficient when we have to fight our way through every progressive step, when new techniques are resisted, when we are forced to over-man new machines?

'Yes, there is some very amateur management in Fleet Street. It is a delicate matter to discuss the management of your opposition, but what appals me is that some of them don't even seem to realize their shortcomings, let alone what they should do about it. Those of your Lordships who saw some of the newspaper proprietors on television, or read their remarks in the papers, must have been just as puzzled as I was. Either they just do not know what is the situation labourwise in their own businesses or they are afraid to tell the truth. I leave it to you to choose which it is.

'Some of those high in the ranks of Labour, and in Government too, have said that I should dig my heels in and refuse unreasonable demands. We did this recently at Hemel Hempstead in a dispute there and this matter has now been satisfactorily resolved. But this was a new venture and I *could* dig my heels in. Let me tell you what the consequences can be now with an existing newspaper if you dig your heels in.

'A few months ago there was a dispute in our press-room between two unions over which man should do which job. This dispute came up unexpectedly. As a result production of the *Sunday Times* was seriously disrupted, and we lost 400,000 copies. That cost us over £40,000 in lost sales, rebates to advertisers, hiring of extra transport because of missed trains, as well as interruption of reading habits of regular customers and resultant loss of goodwill.

'When we are confronted with a last-minute demand

212

for more money, however unreasonable it might be, that would cost us less perhaps than £1,000, whereas to miss a single issue of the *Sunday Times* would involve a loss of £150,000, what are we expected to do? It is all right to be a martyr, but one cannot be at that kind of cost. It is easy to accuse management of giving in too easily to unreasonable demands, but remember that the reading life of a newspaper is only a few hours. Most of the expenses go on whether or not the paper comes out, and revenue lost can never be regained; whereas loss of production in almost any other kind of business can nearly always be recovered when work is resumed.

'There seems to be a general agreement to deplore the possibility of closure of more newspapers. In this I heartily concur. I agree that in a democracy the people should have access to a variety of opinions. There is another reason why I, and I think all other newspaper proprietors, do not welcome closures. Newspapers as a group are competing for advertising revenue with other media. Every newspaper has advantages for advertising certain products and services. But if the choice of news- papers is too limited they are likely to opt for other media, and this would weaken newspapers in general as a dominant advertising medium. I do not want any existing newspaper to cease publication and I will do anything in reason to support this statement. I would point out, in proof of this, the generous concessions—and they were very generous concessions—that I made to *The Observer* and *The Guardian* in connection with *The Times* deal. But this does not prevent me from facing the facts and saying that the conclusions reached in the Report regarding likely closures are, in my opinion, correct.

'What can be done about weak newspapers? They must get more revenue and/or cut their expenses. Obviously if expenses can be cut some at least of the newspapers will be saved. Both *The Guardian* and *The*

Sun will carry on if they can make savings which they specify. They should be given every opportunity to make these savings. If substantial savings can be effected other fringe newspapers can carry on, I hope, always in the hope that revenue can be improved. How can they get more income? Our experience shows that there is always more advertising to be obtained if you have facts and figures to prove to advertisers that your rates are economic for their particular product. This requires research and planning, and it requires strong selling. When a newspaper gets more advertising it does not necessarily come from other newspapers. There are many other media to draw from, but it requires forceful selling. Compared to Canada and the United States, we have not yet reached anything like an optimum level [in this country].

'It is sometimes said that if other newspaper closures take place there will not be enough left to give full scope to differing opinions. How many is "enough"? Nowhere in these islands can there be fewer than ten dailies—and in many places eleven—on the breakfast table every morning, with a similar number of Sunday papers. My Lords, are so many papers really needed? Everywhere there is a local daily available to supplement the nationals; and if, as I fear and the Report indicates, the number of dailies were to be reduced even to four nationals and one or two locals, a choice of five or six would still be more than is available in other democratic countries. In Canada there is no city with more than one morning newspaper with the exception of Montreal, where there are French and English language papers. In the United States, New York has two; Los Angeles one; Philadelphia one; Chicago two and Boston two. I think that every other city in the United States has only one, and where that happens there is no access to any other newspaper. As one noble lord said (I think it was Lord Carrington) they do not seem to suffer under that condition; they seem to be as fully informed as people here. I wonder, when people talk about enough newspapers, how many is "enough"?

'It is very easy to strike a moral attitude when you have no responsibility and when your only concern is to put other people right. It is very easy to say that it would be a national catastrophe if this or that newspaper were obliged to close down. But surely the best judges of that are the readers of the newspaper in question, and the best measure of the strength of their feelings on the subject is what they are prepared to do about it. If its selling price were increased by, say, 3*d*. a copy, would they go on buying it? If so, the troubles of every ailing newspaper would be over. And 3*d*. is not a large sum of money. It is the price of one cigarette, or half the price of a cup of tea in a cheap café, or one-sixth of the price of a pint of beer. Yet if the readers of a newspaper were not prepared to demonstrate in this small way their judgement of its value to them, by what right can the newspaper itself claim to be treated as a social service and subsidized at the expense of its more successful competitors?

'*The Guardian* recently underlined the contrast between freedom and feather-bedding—though it probably did so unintentionally—when it declared:

"Market economics, if allowed to operate as at present, will eventually deprive more readers of the papers of their choice . . . Even when more than a million readers vote with their pennies, as was the case with the *News Chronicle* and is now the case with *The Sun*, the market proves them wrong."

My Lords, this is nonsense. How positively can a paper be a paper of their choice if an increase of 1*d*., 2*d*. or even 3*d*. can lead them to abandon it and read another one? Is

H   215

this the extent of their loyalty, of the way in which it is filling their needs? Can these sums of money be so significant, in a country where the average family income is over £25 a week, that the middle classes who read *The Guardian* . . . would switch to a paper they did not really want in order to save a few coppers a week? And if this is so, how seriously can they be said to want the first one?

'Various suggestions have been put forward for penalizing successful newspapers in order to feather-bed the unsuccessful. It seems a little ironic, at a time when the printing unions are being sharply criticized for their restrictive practices and for attempting to preserve outmoded patterns of newspaper production, that changes in the pattern of the public's newspaper needs, arising inevitably as a result of modern changes in technology and social organisation, should be regarded as tragedies to be averted at all cost. If the readers of an unsuccessful paper are not prepared to vote it an extra penny or two to keep it in existence, who shall decree that more successful newspapers shall be penalized and thus forced to give a worsened service to their readers? Would not this be an intolerable example of job-protecting restrictive practice of the sort which is so much deplored?

'In the preface to the E.I.U. Survey, Lord Devlin says:

"If the present trend continues the forecast is that before this decade ends three more national dailies and one more national Sunday will have gone. They will not be swallowed up by tycoons anxious to foist their own brands of politics on increasing masses. There are no such people. The Report destroys utterly the idea that newspapers can be kept alive by anti-monopoly legislation."

This is very significant. This is the conclusion that was reached after careful investigation. And it is so true. The amalgamations, the consolidations, and takeovers that take place are all a rationalizing process to make the newspaper business more efficient and to ensure their viability against other advertising media like television and magazines.

'Many suggestions have been made regarding Government help or interference . . . I am opposed to anything of this kind. I am sure that if the Government did extend assistance to newspapers they would do it in such a way that there would be no pressure on the newspapers to favour them. I would concede that. However, no company or industry can accept help without placing itself under an obligation. I am sure this would be viewed in foreign countries as an abridgement of the freedom of the press in Britain. We just cannot afford to have this happen. If such help or assistance should come about, I assume that everyone in the business would be treated the same. I hope it does not come about but if it did, I hope it would not be a case of bonusing the inefficient and penalizing the efficient. If this should happen it would presage the beginning of the end of the complete freedom of newspapers as it now exists.

'The suggestion has been made that the Government should set up a printing plant where new newspapers can be printed without the huge investment that is usually required. There is no need for this. I have a plant with large capacity and I make this offer. I will print any new paper without profit, at cost only. That is a standing offer. I would expect that anyone who wants to take advantage of this offer should be adequately financed to ensure that they could carry on at least for a reasonable time, because you get some crackpot schemes coming up. They would have to have enough money to ensure that they would be in business for at least a few months.

'Then again it is suggested that through control of advertising, less should go to the successful papers and more be forced towards the inefficient and unsuccessful. This just would not work. Advertisers do not have to place their advertisements in newspapers. There are other alternative media, and rather than patronize newspapers which they consider would not give them value for their money, they would divert the money in other ways—television, magazines; perhaps into premiums, because that is a possibility; or fancy packaging; posters; window displays; and the multitude of other methods which may be used to assist in the selling of goods.

'It is my opinion that any interference in the free flow of advertising and the ability of advertisers to use the newspaper of their choice would simply reduce the volume in the successful newspapers and in many cases make them in turn unsuccessful, and would not really benefit the weak papers at all. The *Sunday Times* relies upon advertising for about 75 per cent of its income. If we produced the *Sunday Times* without advertising we should have to sell the paper at over two shillings a copy. [Today, in 1975, the price for an average-sized *Sunday Times* and magazine would have to be 45p.] If prices were raised to that extent, circulations would plummet and the British public would have access to less news and fewer opinions than is now the case.

'There has been much talk about what is called the undue dependence of newspapers on advertising revenue. It would be catastrophic if your lordships were to overlook the basic role played by advertising in a free economy dedicated to the concept of the consumer choice, in permitting the manufacturer and the retailer to inform the public of the goods they have for sale and even to try to persuade them of the virtue of these goods. Advertising, as we know it today, is an essential component of an efficient distribution system. And it is no coincidence that it is most highly developed in those countries with the highest standard of living. Modern techniques of management and research have increased its precision enormously during the past few decades, and the suggestion that the advertiser should be prevented from using it in the most efficient way by complicated regulations devised to subsidize newspapers which are no longer viable in their own right, either because they have outlived their function or because they are badly managed, is most inappropriate to the age of technology.

'In some quarters the view seems to be taken that while advertising is a necessary evil it is still an evil, and that newspapers would be better newspapers if they could manage without it. This is arrant nonsense. The highly sophisticated scientific research carried out by my organisation—and by other publishing houses—into the reading habits of the public and the needs which newspapers fill, shows very clearly that from the reader's point of view the advertising is an integral part of the paper, highly valued in its own right and, in some instances, of greater interest to the reader of the paper than parts of the editorial content itself.

'The function of the newspaper as a marketplace for goods and services is just as important a contribution to the modern social and economic organisation as the reporting of parliamentary debates or speculation about the matrimonial and extra-marital affairs of "pop" idols; and to suggest that freedom in one function should be curtailed in order to promote greater diversity in the other implies a very odd set of values. Newspapers create their own personalities and find their own individual levels and characteristics of audiences, which in turn determine the volume and nature of the advertising which finds its way to them. In this way the common will of the community can determine which newspapers it wants to continue and which it does not, and what particular role it wants each of them to fill. I do not see that any case can be made out for riding roughshod over the common will by penalizing the successful newspaper in favour of the unsuccessful—that is to say by imposing upon the population a newspaper structure different from that which they would choose for themselves.

' . . . Whether you regard the newspaper industry as simply a business like any other, or whether you feel there is something special about it, it is an inescapable fact that the operation of a modern newspaper is a complex matter involving the most highly specialized management, technical and commercial considerations not comprehended by the general public or, for that matter, by many newspaper workers and, I am afraid, not by all newspaper owners. A man may be a good dramatic critic or cookery expert, or even gossip columnist, without understanding the working of the industry.

' . . . The worth-while newspapers will continue and some of them will prosper. By and large, I think that those newspapers will survive which best serve their communities and whose businesses are well conducted. Those factors inevitably go together.'

INDEX

INDEX

King, Cecil, 95–102, 111, 163, 168, 169
Kosygin, Alexei N., 136
Kraus, Hans, 147
Kraus-Thomson, 147

Labour News, 113
Langton, Captain Teddy, 151, 152
Lardner-Burke, D. W., 195
Law, James, 18–19
Lee, Mrs., 86, 87, 88–9, 91
Littler, Prince, 51
Living, 164
Logan, Jimmy, 44, 50
Lord, Cyril, 85

MacAlister, Bob, 206
McCabe, St. Clair, 25, 35, 117
Macdonald, Ian, 46–7, 50, 64, 65, 66
Macdonald, Sir Peter, 50
Mackenzie, Sir Compton, 42, 50
Mackinnon, Colin, 7, 8, 9–10, 12, 15
Mackintosh of Mackintosh, 43
McMaster, D. W., 86, 88, 89, 92
Macmillan, Harold, 98, 100, 131, 132, 145
McMunagle, 'Wullie', 32–4
McNeil, Hector, 43
McQueen, Charles, 44, 50, 63
McVeigh, Mr. Justice, 93–4
Mathers, Lady, 45, 50
Matthew, Francis, 167, 168
Meagan, Mrs., 113
Men's Wear, 111
Miami Herald, 186
Miller, Jack, 25
Montgomery, Viscount, 193
Morison, Stanley, 167
Muir, James, 11, 20–21
Munro, Ian, 15, 16, 25, 60, 62–3
Munro, J. H. B., 50
Murdoch, Rupert, 83
Mussolini, Benito, 163–4

Nanaimo Free Press, 31
Nasser, Gamal Abdel, 144
National Commercial Bank of Scotland, 47
National Graphical Association (NGA), 155–8, 183–4, 188–90
National Society of Operative Printers and Assistants (NATSOPA), 155–8, 183, 189–90
Neale, Charles A., 50
Nehru, Pandit, 137–8
Nelson, Thomas, and Sons Ltd., 112, 115–16
News of the World, 84, 100

Nixon, Richard, 143
Noble, John, 9, 15, 74
North Sea Oil consortium, 200–7
Nyerere, Julius, 195

Observer, 213
Occidental Oil, 199–203, 206
Odhams, 80, 110, 111; abortive moves for merger with, 95–102, 110, 121
Outram, George, and Co., 43–4, 59, 62

Palmar, Derek, 97
Pappas, George, 160–1
Parnell, Val, 51
Parrack, Geoffrey, 111, 164
People, The, 98, 99
Perry, Geoffrey, 164
Pick, Charles, 112
Pope, Sir George, 168
Press Conference television interview, 128–9
Profumo, John, 45, 50
Purdy, Rai, 45, 50, 55

Radcliffe, Jack, 44, 50
Rainbird, George, 140
Raitz, Vladimir, 150
Rankin, Mr. (solicitor), 91
Reading *Evening Post*, 154
Rees-Mogg, William, 179
Renshaw, Michael, 72, 126
Richards, Edgar, 172
Riviera Holidays, 152
Robens, Lord, 179
Roll, Sir Eric, 179
Rosebery, Lord, 43
Roskill, A. W., 171
Rothermere, Lord, 82, 95, 100, 153, 165

Saxone Shoe Co., 15
Sayers, J. E., 87, 94
Sayers, R. M., 87, 88, 90, 93
Scotsman, 65, 131, 191, 204; purchase of, 1, 4–21, 40; changes in, 22–9, 74; financial problems, 24–5, 34–9
Scotsman Publications Ltd., 7, 12, 204
Scottish Television Ltd., 41–57, 63, 64, 65, 108, 148
Self-Help (Smiles), 107–8
Shard, Charles, 95, 96
Shawcross, Lord, 179
Sky Tours, 151–2
Smiles, Samuel, 107, 114
Snowdon, Lord, 122–4
Stacey, Tom, 126

INDEX

Star, The, 166
Stevenson, Sir Edward, 31–2, 41, 42, 46, 50
Stewart, Sir Ian M., 50
Stewart, Michael, 200
Sun, The, 214, 215
Sunday Express, 122
Sunday Graphic, 77
Sunday Telegraph, 79, 82
Sunday Times, 98, 131, 143, 162, 191, 193, 212–13, 218; purchase of, 60, 61–75; changes in, 73; printed at Gray's Inn Road, 76–82; book publishing with *Time Life,* 109; Colour Magazine, 121–8, 134, 180; and *The Times,* 165, 166–80

Thomson, Edna Alice, 2, 3–4, 8, 27, 208
Thomson, Kenneth, 4, 8, 15, 21, 31, 34, 126, 132, 140, 171, 173, 175, 180, 202
Thomson British Holdings Ltd., 50
Thomson Company of Canada Ltd., 12
Thomson Directories (Yellow Pages) Ltd., 149–50, 153
Thomson Foundation, 196–7
Thomson Holidays, 150–3
Thomson International, 147
Thomson Newspapers Ltd., diversification of, 108–16
Thomson Printers Ltd., 109
Thomson Publications, diversification of, 111–16, 146–64
Thomson Scottish Associates, 65, 174, 201, 202
Thomson Scottish Petroleum Ltd., 29, 203–7

Time Life, 109
Times, The, 23, 102, 143, 187, 213; acquisition of, 165–81; move to Gray's Inn Road, 179–80
Times Newspapers Ltd., 171, 174, 180
Tito, President, 137
Tyerman, Donald, 172

United Newspapers, 37, 38, 39

Video Display Terminals (VDTs), 186
Vorster, B. J., 138–9

Wagg, Helbert, 60, 63, 64
Warburg, S. G., 60, 63–4, 70, 200–201
Wason, Eugene, 94, 194–5
Waterhouse, Keith, 84, 129
Watson, Murray, 19, 22, 23, 28
Weekly Scotsman, 12
Weir, Lord, 43
Wheadon, Ivor, 71, 78, 80–1
Whitton, James, 9–11, 13, 14, 32, 42, 50
Wilkinson, Mrs., 88, 90
Williams, J. A. D., 152
Wilson, Harold, 144
Woodcock, George, 99, 157–8, 189
Wright, Rev. Selby, 29
Wyndham, John, 172

Yamey, Professor B. S., 172
Yarrow, Sir Harold, 43
Yellow Pages, 149–50, 153

Zhivkov, Zhivko, 137